Experiencing the Abundance
of the Spirit

Step
into the Waters

Rita J. Platt

NAVPRESS

NAVPRESS

NavPress is the publishing ministry of The Navigators, an international Christian organization and leader in personal spiritual development. NavPress is committed to helping people grow spiritually and enjoy lives of meaning and hope through personal and group resources that are biblically rooted, culturally relevant, and highly practical.

For a free catalog go to www.NavPress.com
or call 1.800.366.7788 in the United States or 1.800.839.4769 in Canada.

ISBN: 978-1-60006-389-3

Cover design by Arvid Wallen
Cover image by Shutterstock

Some of the anecdotal illustrations in this book are true to life and are included with the permission of the persons involved. All other illustrations are composites of real situations, and any resemblance to people living or dead is coincidental.

Unless otherwise identified, all Scripture quotations in this publication are taken from the *Holy Bible, New International Version* (NIV). Copyright © 1973, 1978, 1984 by International Bible Society. Used by permission of Zondervan. All rights reserved. Other versions used include: *THE MESSAGE* (MSG). Copyright © 1993, 1994, 1995, 1996, 2000, 2001, 2002. Used by permission of NavPress Publishing Group; and the *Amplified Bible* (AMP), © The Lockman Foundation 1954, 1958, 1962, 1964, 1965, 1987.

Printed in the United States of America

1 2 3 4 5 6 7 8 / 13 12 11 10 09

For Thom

For the waterfall moments; you always encourage me to

dive in deeper.

Also by Rita J. Platt:

I Am His

An Undivided Heart

Contents

Acknowledgments

I'm deeply grateful to Chris Sabin. Over the years, your friendship has drawn me deeper. Thank you for the many long phone conversations, hearing my heart, and helping me embrace life.

To my sons—Josh, Jim, and Jon—I love you. Thank you for playing in the sprinklers and for prodding me to jump into adventure headfirst. Also, I'm grateful to the many friends and family who have listened to my excitement and encouraged me along the way.

I'm forever indebted to the professors and students at Denver Seminary who so willingly shared their lives with me. You nurtured and challenged my heart and my mind. Thank you for showing me that abundant life is meant to be lived from the inside out.

Throughout the writing of this study, I felt the impact of watching a loved one struggle with chronic disease. So many churches and prayer teams faithfully lifted me to the Lord. Thank you to Woodmen Valley Chapel (especially the choir and worship arts team), Christ the King, Living Hope, and Emmanuel Baptist. You demonstrated the love of the Lord to me.

Over the years, I've enjoyed reading many NavPress books. I can't express what it means to me to work with a publisher I've admired for so long. I'm honored to have Rebekah Guzman as my editor and to partner with the excellent team at NavPress.

And finally, Thom, I don't know how to thank you. You've been there when I've bounced around in excitement over a new idea, held me when I've grieved, and encouraged me when I've been scared to death. God gave me an incredible gift in you.

Immersed in Life

We are triple-kept by triune love, shielded by the three in one.

— CALVIN MILLER

Sitting on the beach can be a spectator sport. On one particular occasion, I watched as men, women, and children ventured into the water in different ways. A young woman got just her toes wet and then saw the fish swimming in the clear waters and ran screaming back onto the beach. The adventurous people took a few steps and dove in. Others inched their way in, inhaling sharply with each step before their skin acclimated to the water temperature. For most, once they were thoroughly wet, the delight began.

I wonder if we at times stand on the banks of living water and scope it out in a similar fashion. We watch some rush headlong toward the river and others stand timidly feeling their way. Those who splash in delight or float calmly might call out, "Come on in; the water's fine." Still others have been shoved in, scaring them and creating fear of the water. Whatever your frame of reference, I pray that our exploration of living waters invites you into the flow of abundant life.

The waters that immerse us in complete love spring from the generous heart of God. He is our perfect Father, our loving Savior, and the life-giving Spirit. As we step into the waters together and let them bathe our spirits, I wish for you the blessings of a deeper intimacy with the Spirit. I'd love to pray in person with each of you, but because I cannot do that, I hope you will receive the Celtic blessing that follows. Try speaking the words aloud, welcoming them into your mind and heart.

The blessings of God be to thee,
The blessings of Christ be to thee,
The blessings of Spirit be to thee,
And to thy children.

To thee and to thy children,
The peace of God be to thee,
The peace of Christ be to thee,
During all thy life,
All the days of thy life.

The keeping of God upon thee in every pass,
The shielding of Christ upon thee in every path,
The bathing of Spirit upon thee in every stream,
In every land and sea thou goest.[1]

Ponder Scripture

The unified love of our triune God flings the door to life wide open. Our Abba Father so desires relationship with us that He sent Jesus to pour out His life in an extravagant act of love, making a way for us to be restored to relationship with God and releasing the Holy Spirit to live within us. We receive life and we're embraced in an eternal circle of love.

Celebrate John 3:16 as you read it aloud from *The Message* translation of the Bible:

This is how much God loved the world: He gave his Son, his one and only Son. And this why: so that no one need be destroyed; by believing in him, anyone can have a whole and lasting life.

Anyone. Life is extended to all of us. It doesn't matter where we've been, who we've been with, or what we've done. When we welcome the love of God, there's nothing—no sense of futility, shame, or even bland existing—big enough to stop the flow of life.

Please read John 4:4-26 taking on the role of the Samaritan woman. As you enter into the story, keep in mind that she went to the well at about noon rather than in the cool of the morning so that she could avoid the other women. She carried shame and deep hurt with her to the well. Bruce Demarest suggested that she's like "a hurting child dressed up in a grown woman's clothes."[2]

In what ways, if any, can you relate to this woman?

Both life and death are written all over this passage. Please read John 4:4-26 again and describe evidence of death in the woman's life.

Next, list or describe the characteristics of the real life Jesus offers.

At first the Samaritan woman fixed her attention on the immediate and tangible realities around her, but Jesus helped her see there was much more to what He was offering. How might Jesus be inviting you to look beyond the physical realm, to connect with life in a deeper way?

Pause and respond honestly to His invitation. Tell Him of your eagerness, delight, or apprehension.

Let's move further on in the book of John to chapter 7, verses 37-39. Hear the words of Jesus as if He were standing in your living room proclaiming them directly to you. Jot down any initial impressions and note how the water is released. What characteristics of water do you notice in your environment? Do you live near a lake, a stream, a river? Or is water scarce? Think about places you've seen and experienced the scent and feel of water. If you could capture living water with a picture, what would it look like as opposed to nonliving water?

We drink of living water the moment we believe, welcoming the life-giving flow of the Holy Spirit in our lives, but it doesn't end there. Max Lucado said, "Jesus employs a verb that suggests repeated swallows. Literally, 'Let him come to me and drink and keep on drinking.' . . . Ceaseless communion satisfies thirsty souls."[3]

Brainstorm ways you could keep drinking as if you were sipping from a water bottle all day long.

An Image of Living Water

Ezekiel 47 paints a powerful picture of living water. Before we dive in, it's helpful to have a little background information. Verses 1 and 12 and Revelation 22:1 identify the source of life-giving water. Commentaries tell us that the "Messiah is the temple and the door; from his pierced side flow the living waters ever increasing both in the individual believer and in the heart."[4] The waters are not fed from any source other than the sanctuary, the throne room, the Lamb of God Himself.

In addition, Ezekiel 40:1-4 sets the stage for the events of Ezekiel 40–48. "The year was 572 B.C. Ezekiel had served as a prophet for about twenty years. God took Ezekiel to Israel to an unnamed high mountain. From there Ezekiel could see God's plans unfold in a vision."[5] Commentators are not in complete agreement about all of the meanings involved in the prophecy of Ezekiel 40–48. There can be here and now and future meanings, corporate and individual meanings.

We will focus simply on the vision revealing the river of life from Ezekiel 47:1-12. Try to set aside the urge to interpret each symbol. Instead, imagine yourself right there with Ezekiel in the midst of this sensory explosion. Feel the water, smell the scents, and see the sights.

What about the river captures your attention? List some of the effects of the water. Which effect most appeals to you today?

Try to identify any other sense in which the waters are personally enticing or invigorating.

Eager Yet Apprehensive

The river of life is beautiful, yet it seems overwhelming at times too. Let's look at a few stories that illustrate some of the barriers people might experience that keep them from diving in.

My Struggle

I sat with a group of musicians in the green room (a place to hang out before going on stage) and grinned, enjoying the friendly banter. Somehow we came to the subject of self-description. Out of my mouth flew a one-word description of my approach to most of life since engaging with Jesus: "eager." That eagerness has sometimes been tamped down by different events in my life. The most powerful deflation device by far has been fear. When I allow fear free rein, apprehension enters in and replaces eagerness. I shy away from the water of life, from the abundant goodness of God's plans for me.

Serena's Story

Serena also feels the life-draining effects of fear. When delving into the spiritual life, she shields her heart from advancing change. She shares how she purposely surrenders to a point and then holds back, even walks away. If a book she's reading begins to challenge her or suggest change in some way, she lays it aside. Serena talks about a fear of what-ifs: *What if I get too demonstrative? What if my personality is robbed?*

What if I'm asked to change something I don't think I can change?

Serena feels as though she creates a safety zone for herself by not fully engaging. She says she wants transformation but is scared and seeks to place limits on surrender.

Nicki's Story

Nicki's response to the mention of living water is to remind me that some like to dip just a toe in here and there. She's not so sure about getting all wet. There's a feeling that this Spirit-filled life could control her or take over so she becomes a nonperson. Nicki experiments with taking in just enough water to add a little hydration but not so much that she fears that her comfort zone will be violated. She keeps up a "No Trespassing" sign on portions of her heart, yet she yearns for more life. She doesn't feel certain it's safe to let down her defenses with the Holy Spirit.

What one word would you use to characterize your approach to life?

If there was a time in your life when you could identify with one of the three stories about barriers to diving into living water, please describe your story.

C. S. Lewis told a fictional story of Jill and Aslan (the Lion) that parallels the three stories. Jill hears the sound of the stream and is nearly overcome by thirst, but she's cautious about approaching the water because Aslan is next to the stream watching her. Jill fights an internal war between self-protection, control, and quenching her thirst with clear, cool water.

 "Are you not thirsty?" said the Lion.

"I'm *dying* of thirst," said Jill.

"Then drink," said the Lion.

"May I — could I — would you mind going away while I do?" said Jill.

The Lion answered this only by a look and a very low growl. And as Jill gazed at its motionless bulk, she realised that she might as well have asked the whole mountain to move aside for her convenience.

The delicious rippling noise of the stream was driving her nearly frantic.

"Will you promise not to — do anything to me, if I do come?" said Jill.

"I make no promise," said the Lion. . . . "I have swallowed up girls and boys, women and men, kings and emperors, cities and realms," said the Lion. It didn't say this as if it were boasting, nor as if it were sorry, nor as if it were angry. It just said it.

"I daren't come and drink," said Jill.

"Then you will die of thirst," said the Lion.

"Oh dear!" said Jill, coming another step nearer. "I suppose I must go and look for another stream then."

"There is no other stream," said the Lion.[6]

Some of us have heard stories or encountered situations that cultivated a fear of the water, but as Aslan told Jill, there is one source alone. Still, the good news is that there is a source.

The Holy Spirit beckons us to look to Him for courage, move even an inch past our fear, and come and drink. His very name inspires trust. He isn't just any spirit — He is the Holy Spirit. He is holy, other, set apart. "The Spirit is not man's own potential, but entirely the gift, the power and strength of God. The Holy Spirit, as God's Spirit, must be distinguished from man's own spirit, since he is the Holy Spirit free from all sin."[7]

Look up the following scriptures and fill in some descriptors of the Holy Spirit.

Scripture Reference	Descriptive Words and Phrases
John 14:16-18,26; 16:12-15	
Romans 5:5	
Romans 8:9	
Romans 8:16; Galatians 4:6	
Romans 8:26-27	
Romans 15:13	
1 Corinthians 2:11	
Ephesians 1:13-14	

Imagine a bottomless glass of each description of the Holy Spirit is sitting before you. Which one do you wish you could gulp down or sip steadily today? Will you take the time to pause and ask for a drink?

One place to begin drinking is in Romans 8:1-17. Read through this passage carefully, drinking in each mention of the Spirit.

Now explore verses 9-11 again, this time from *The Message*:

If God himself has taken up residence in your life, you can hardly be thinking more of yourself than of him. Anyone, of course, who has not welcomed this invisible but clearly present God, the Spirit of Christ, won't know what we're talking about. But for you who welcome him, in whom he dwells—even though you still experience all the limitations of sin—you yourself experience life on God's terms. It stands to reason, doesn't it, that if the alive-and-present God who raised Jesus from the dead moves into your life, he'll do the same thing in you that he did in Jesus, bringing you alive to himself? When God lives and breathes in you (and he does, as surely as he did in Jesus), you are delivered from that dead life. With his Spirit living in you, your body will be as alive as Christ's!

Bring any thoughts, questions, or insights prompted by this passage to the Lord, forming them into a prayer.

With the scriptures in the chart fresh in your mind, return to Ezekiel 47:1-12 and read about the river of life once again. The depths may appear both welcoming and scary at the same time. Ultimately, they are good. The water teems with life. Ask God for the courage to brave the waters even when it means venturing into the unknown. What might it look like for you to plunge a little further into life today?

Reflect

Wherever the river flows, life will flourish . . . Where the river flows, life abounds.

— EZEKIEL 47:9, MSG

In the movie *Secondhand Lions*, Walter is a boy desperate for something solid and true to believe. His mother made a habit of lying to him and abandoning him. This time she leaves him with his great uncles. Walter hears stories of their worldwide adventures and, wide-eyed yet wounded, longs to believe them. He is an adult when his uncles die and comes to see the wreckage of the plane they tried to fly upside down through a barn. As he stands shaking his head, a helicopter lands and a man and his son step down. A look of wonder crosses Walter's face when he learns they are descended from a sheik, a main character in his uncles' stories. When the young son realizes that the uncles were real men, he asks, "You mean they really lived?" Walter answers, "Yeah, they *really* lived."[8]

What would it look like for you to *really* live?

Choose one of the following exercises to experiment with this week:

* Describe someone who you believe really lives? How does that person ooze life?
* Play with watercolors. Notice how water flows through every color. Create something titled "Life Flow" or another title of your choosing.
* Consider how you can become aware of life flowing through you in the ordinary, exciting, and tranquil moments of your day. Use your day planner or Post-it notes to write messages of life. You could write a scripture that shouts "Life" to you in different time slots of your day planner, put it on your computer desktop, or post it on the refrigerator. Every time you see the scripture, let it focus your heart on the intimate life of Christ living in and through you.
* When you take a shower, wash your hands, watch or feel the rain, turn on a faucet, or get a drink, be aware of the water. Think about how water flows, how it goes places that solid substances cannot penetrate. With every water encounter, pray for living water to penetrate every relationship, task, and moment of your day. At the end of the week, jot down any thoughts you have about what you've experienced.

Respond

Real life is evidence of communion with the Lord. It flows outward even when we live and walk among the stench of decay. Life keeps streaming because its source is inexhaustible. Oswald Chambers wrote, "In the life of a saint there is this amazing Well, which is a continual Source of original life. The Spirit of God is a Well of water springing up perpetually fresh."[9]

Living water is never stagnant or stale. The Holy Spirit invites us to drink it in and rejoice as the very life of God flows through us. Isaiah 12:3-5 exclaims,

> Joyfully you'll pull up buckets of water
>   from the wells of salvation.
> And as you do it, you'll say,
>   "Give thanks to GOD.
> Call out his name.
>   Ask him anything!
> Shout to the nations, tell them what he's done,
>   spread the news of his great reputation!
>
> "Sing praise-songs to GOD. He's done it all!
>   Let the whole earth know what he's done!
> Raise the roof! Sing your hearts out, O Zion!
>   The Greatest lives among you: The Holy of Israel." (MSG)

Only the Author of life is able to make life spring up within you regardless of your surroundings, wherever you've been, whatever you're facing. Bring your brokenness, your celebrations, all of who you are to Him and sing your heart out.

Conclude this week's study with this prayer song:

Only You pour peace over me,
Like water kissing rock;
Only You form pools of holy love,
Soaking every crevice in my heart.
Only You bathe my soul in grace
Like an ever-flowing stream;
Only You make life well up in me
Washing away fear, setting me free.
Immerse me, Lord, immerse me,
Cover me with only You.
Immerse me, Lord, immerse me,
I'll rest immersed in only You.

Running On Empty

See that lemon on the windowsill? That lemon has been cut in half, squeezed, all the juice has come out of it, and it's just dried up. That's what we're like.
— HUNGARIAN LEADER, 1989

In a scene of the movie *Ben Hur*, Judah Ben-Hur is wrung out and ready to collapse. He's being marched to serve a sentence rowing aboard a Roman ship. On the way, staggering with weariness and thirst, he becomes desperate for a drink. He and the others slop water all over themselves and the ground in their desperation. Just as the dipper is finally raised to his lips, it's dashed away by a guard. You can see all hope drain from him. Then a man (the movie's representation of Jesus) serves Judah water, holds the vessel for him, and tenderly refreshes his thirst. As Judah looks into the eyes of this man and thanks him, he is momentarily invigorated and able to go on.

I've seen that same beseeching gaze in the eyes of a woman as she shared her hurts with me, that look that says, "I'm hanging on by a thread to hope for refreshing." She stood poised to keep walking, but every move unveiled her thirst. She was parched and drained by daily battles in her life, and her entire countenance shouted her urgency to soothe the dry aching of her spirit. The very second a cup of thirst-quenching hope was in sight, she tried to keep her reserve but lunged for it, taking in what she could and letting the rest run down her face.

When was the last time you felt desperately dry? If there are arid places in your spirit today, pour out your need here.

Write a prayer inviting the Holy Spirit to meet you in your need. Tell Him where you feel dry or weary and let Him hold the cup of life to your parched lips.

If you're not experiencing dryness right now, write a prayer thanking Him for moisturizing your heart and looking forward to daily renewal.

Ponder Scripture

In Psalm 63:1 David called out,

> O God, you are my God,
>   earnestly I seek you;
> my soul thirsts for you,
>   my body longs for you,
> in a dry and weary land
>   where there is no water.

What dry and weary places have you wandered around recently or in the past? List what tends to drain or deplete your spirit.

There have been periods of my life when I've felt dry and weary. I struggled to get through the day, just going through the motions and wondering why I couldn't muster up the "right" attitude. I felt as if my legs were stuck in a swamp while the rest of me kept trying to move on. I'm so grateful that in those times, the Holy Spirit beckoned me, and even carried me, to the water.

One time in particular stands out. There were family issues to deal with and church functions to attend. I'd been working hard, hearing the drought in others' lives, feeling their thirst, crying over them, and pouring out everything I had, hoping they'd catch a few drops of life. But I soon found myself wrung out and so weary that I didn't know if I could continue absorbing pain for even one more day.

I sensed the call to return to and focus on the Source of my life. In my mind's eye, I knew it was as if the Lord was cupping my chin in His hand, tilting my head back, taking a pitcher of living water, and pouring it into me. The sweet refreshing impact of that image loosened my tears and they began to mingle with the water. That day, the dry lands developing in my spirit were replaced with a flow of life, renewal, and energy to live, even in the midst of drought.

Scripture describes the flow of life that envelops the dry places. Please read Ezekiel 47:8-9 and Jeremiah 17:5-8. Note the characteristics of the salt lands. What brings transformation to the salt lands? What shape do the salt lands take in your life?

The apostle Paul knew the threat of becoming drained. He was no stranger to relationship challenges, disappointment, physical pain, rejection, weariness, and heartache, yet he experienced the indwelling Spirit transforming the ordinary to the extraordinary, the natural to the supernatural.

Please read 2 Corinthians 4:7-9. Then list the harsh challenges Paul's body, soul, and heart were subjected to and also what he was saved from.

Harsh Challenges	But Saved From . . .

Read 2 Corinthians 4:7-9 once again from *The Message* and add any additional insights to your list.

If you only look at *us*, you might well miss the brightness. We carry this precious Message around in the unadorned clay pots of our ordinary lives. That's to prevent anyone from confusing God's incomparable power with us. As it is, there's not much chance of that. You know for yourselves that we're not much to look at. We've been surrounded and battered by troubles, but we're not demoralized; we're not sure what to do, but we know that God knows what to do; we've been spiritually terrorized, but God hasn't left our side; we've been thrown down, but we haven't broken.

Which aspect of Paul's experience could you most identify with over the last few years? Use the following table to track some of those challenges, celebrating any deliverance that has come.

Three to Five Years Ago	One Year Ago	In the Past Month

Renee's Story

Renee was walking through a time most would expect to be a salt land, a time of great physical pain and discouragement. Serious and chronic health problems were cropping up, and just when she thought she had an answer, a new development popped up and changed the whole picture. When she spoke with me, she reminded me that she expected trouble here on earth, that she believed in eternity, that she knew the indwelling Lord of life, and that peace flowed through her spirit in ways never experienced before. She dropped living water on me, though she was in the midst of turmoil.

Renee knew the truth Paul discovered and wrote about in 2 Corinthians 4:16-18. It is the truth that holds our hand and stills our soul, the truth that takes over in the midst of everyday tiredness and earth-shaking blows, the truth the Spirit dips us in and pours into us as He propels us onward to the day of ultimate renewal.

> We're not giving up. How could we! Even though on the outside it often looks like things are falling apart on us, on the inside, where God is making new life, not a day goes by without his unfolding grace. These hard times are small potatoes compared to the coming good times, the lavish celebration prepared for us. There's far more here than meets the eye. The things we see now are here today, gone tomorrow. But the things we can't see now will last forever. (MSG)

Think about one challenge, gigantic or bite-sized, you are currently facing. Sit quietly before the Holy Spirit and ask for inward grace and eternal perspective. In your journal jot down any thoughts that come, and commit to act on any insight you are given.

Soaking in Daily Renewal

Have you ever lived in an area where droughts are common? It's amazing what happens when there's a sudden and immense downpour. The ground is so parched that some of the water just runs off. What is needed is a weather system that produces a soaking rain, steady precipitation that sometimes lasts for hours, even days. The water needs time to settle into the cracked earth and seep down deep, preparing the surface to drink in the moisture.

In the 2 Corinthians passage, Paul talked about daily renewal. We need regular infusions of living water to stay hydrated. Sadly, for some that concept has taken on the form of obligatory daily readings, of just getting through and checking off daily Scripture reading. Some have shared the guilt they feel when they don't complete a religious checklist each day. They talk about hurrying through, skimming daily readings to be able to say, "See, I've completed my religious duty."

While I'm not knocking daily disciplines, as they are very important in my life, I do hope for more than a life like Steve Martin's character described in the movie *Parenthood*. During a high-stress time and a fight with his wife, he says, "My whole life is 'have to.'"[1] Studying God's Word doesn't have to equate to drudgery. Some days, reading the Word may seem like a task to complete, but hopefully there are also times of enjoyment as we soak in the life of Scripture.

In John 6:63, Jesus told us, "The Spirit gives life; the flesh counts for nothing. The words I have spoken to you are spirit and they are life." The Spirit pulses life through every word God speaks. Too often I miss the delight of absorbing wonder, of tasting living water, because I live like a piece of music with no rests. I rush through without letting the impact of the words saturate my spirit. I forget to carve out space for soaking.

Turn to Deuteronomy 32:2 and read it aloud, savoring it as you might a walk in a gentle rain or a time of catching snowflakes on your tongue. Take your time and picture each image. Feel the water as it falls. How might you be affected if the Holy Spirit were to pour the Word of God on your heart in this way?

Thirst-Quenching Practice

As the Spirit showers us with living water, one way to get wet through and through is to engage in the practice of meditation. When we meditate, we're empowered to step away from our busyness, hurried pace, or any other drying agents and drink deeply of God's Word. "Meditation is a long ardent gaze at God, his work, and his Word. Slowing down and giving one's undivided attention to God lies at the core of Christian meditation."[2] It is mentioned more than fifty times in the Old Testament.[3] As we meditate on Scripture, the Holy Spirit engages us on every level, helping us personally receive the thirst-quenching Word of God. Dietrich Bonhoeffer put it this way:

 In our meditation we ponder the promise that it has something utterly personal to say to us today and for our Christian life, that it is not only God's Word for the Church but also God's Word for us individually. We expose ourselves to the specific word until it addresses us personally. And when we do this, we are doing no more than the simplest, untutored Christian does every day; we read God's Word as God's Word for us.[4]

Look up a sampling of the verses that refer to meditation and identify the role of meditation in the psalmist's life:

- ◆ Psalm 1:2 _____
- ◆ Psalm 19:14 _____
- ◆ Psalm 77:12 _____
- ◆ Psalm 104:34 _____
- ◆ Psalm 119:15 _____

Which aspect of meditation are you most drawn to?

Take a few minutes to write about a time God's Word personally refreshed you. If you cannot recall a specific time, dream on paper what it might be like.

Soak It In

Turn to Isaiah 40:28-31. Before reading the passage, ask the Holy Spirit to let the Word of God rain down and sink in, replenishing the aquifer of your soul. Ask Him to bring the passage alive. Read the passage silently and then out loud.

Pause and sit quietly for a few minutes, and then read the passage again. What word or phrase are you drawn to?

Consider taking a meditative walk. Ask the Holy Spirit to let the phrase repeat in your mind or echo in your heart, to let it become part of your motion or the rhythm of your spirit as you walk. When you return, reread the passage one more time, letting the words wash over your heart.

How is the Holy Spirit at work in you through Isaiah 40:28-31? In what way might He be teaching you, imploring you, strengthening you, or inviting you? Take a few moments to respond with a word, a picture, a thought, or an impression.

Splashing in Renewal

One of my favorite photos is of my twins playing in the sprinklers on a hot day. The glee stretching from their squeals to the animation of their bodies makes me wish I'd joined them. What was the last thing you saw or did that birthed laughter or the kind of smile that reaches all the way to your eyes?

Play renews and recreates eternal perspective. Author Mark Buchanan suggested that "play is subversive. It hints at a world beyond us. . . . When we play, we nudge the border of forever."[5] He drew attention to the following scene from C. S. Lewis's *The Lion, the Witch, and the Wardrobe*:

 "Oh, children catch me if you can!" He stood for a second, his eyes very bright, his limbs quivering, lashing himself with his tail. Then he made a leap high over their heads and landed on the other side of the Table. Laughing, though she didn't know why, Lucy scrambled over it to reach him. Aslan leaped again. A mad chase began. Round and round the hilltop he led them, now hopelessly out of their reach, now letting them almost catch his tail, now diving between them, now tossing them in the air with his huge and beautifully velveted paws and catching them again, and now stopping unexpectedly so that all three of them rolled over together in a happy laughing heap of fur and arms and legs. It was such a romp as no one has ever had except in Narnia: and whether it was more like playing with a thunderstorm or playing with a kitten Lucy could never make up her mind. And the funny thing was that when all three finally lay together panting in the sun the girls no longer felt in the least tired or hungry or thirsty.[6]

What desires, if any, are created in you when you read a scene like this one?

Be alert throughout the week for opportunities to play. Try to describe what it could look like for the Holy Spirit to lead you in a time of play, of laughter and delight in the Lord, and then open yourself to welcome such an experience.

Reflect

I remembered the old days,
    went over all you've done, pondered the ways you've worked,
Stretched out my hands to you,
    as thirsty for you as a desert thirsty for rain.

— PSALM 143:5-6, MSG

There's an old hymn that exhorts, "Count your blessings, name them one by one, count your blessings, see what God has done."[7] Carve out some time to think about the people, events, Scripture verses, music, artwork, and experiences with nature that bless and refresh your spirit.

Then consider experimenting with one or more of these exercises:

1. Mark each section in the following chart with a color designated for each category (use crayons, pen, or any other coloring utensil you can find). Make a mark or symbol for each person, event, and so forth that you can think of. Then step back and survey the colors. Ask the Holy Spirit to fill your hungering spirit with God's goodness as you reflect on the myriad of ways He's revealed Himself in your life.

People	Events	Scriptures	Music	Artwork	Nature

2. Make a blessings poster. You could create a table listing each blessing with a different color, use symbols for different ways God has worked in your life, or make a collage.

3. Create an abstract piece of art representing the intermingling of blessings. Use a different color for each category or design a symbol that prompts you to remember the ways God has refreshed your life with His presence.

When you finish your chosen exercise, write a prayer in your journal asking the Holy Spirit to jog your memory with the wonder and gratitude as you walk through the coming days. Ask Him to drench your spirit with the colors you discovered and to fortify you for future times when drought threatens to conquer and shrivel your spirit.

Respond

Above all else, guard your heart,
for it is the wellspring of life.

— PROVERBS 4:23

May the Holy Spirit shower you with life, hope, and energy. If your ground is parched today, may He invade and saturate it as you place yourself regularly in His refreshing presence. Like keeping that cool clear bottle of water available to stay hydrated, respond to and intentionally receive the ongoing influx of the Holy Spirit.

On our journey, we go "from strength to strength" (Psalm 84:7) as we lean into our eternal destiny. What kind of strength stops have you built into the rhythm of your life? Where are the water stations?

Think through the rhythm of your week, the regular highs and lows of your days, and useful tools for freshening up your spirit. Then take some time to journal and create a plan for regular renewal.

When you do engage in times of retreat, you might wish to prepare by gathering a few items. In addition to a Bible, a writing utensil, and a journal, author Jennifer Kennedy Dean suggested the following:

- Devotional book
- Sketch pad and pencils
- Worshipful music and something to play it on
- Recordings of nature sounds
- Candles
- A hymn or chorus book[8]

What would you add to or subtract from this list?

How can you build daily retreat time as well as more extended retreat times into your life?

If you already have a plan in place, use this time to review or revise it. Then, commit the elements of your plan to the Lord, asking Him to give you intentionality and flexibility.

Please pray with me and continue in your own words as you feel led:

> *Holy Spirit, gather together the details of this plan and refine it; infuse it with life. Sometimes I have retreat time built into my schedule and then circumstances pop up, diverting my attention and rearranging my day. Keep me close when discouragement threatens to overwhelm me. In the midst of those hectic days, show me how to drink deeply of the water of life. Draw me to Yourself; refresh and fill my heart anew.*

Creating Radiance

The Holy Spirit calls forth from us all that is nurturing and intuitive.

— Madeleine L'Engle

A phone call across the country to a friend created freshness and changed my day. She always seemed to get what lingered under the surface of my words. I'd been trying to keep all things in motion, to keep life looking normal when it was anything but normal. Our conversation created in me the ability to breathe, to drink deeply, and to keep moving but with authenticity.

Another woman, Trish, experienced newness when she saw the ultrasound of her baby. That picture was so much more than an image of a baby; it was a picture of God's creative handiwork, of life. When Trish saw her baby, the love created in her went so deep it was fused with her soul.

When or where have you seen or experienced the creative force of love?

Sometimes in the creative process, something gets sloughed off. What might have been shed to make room for newness in the above-mentioned examples or in your own experience?

What is your first response to the possibility of opening your heart to the creativity of the Holy Spirit?

Consider sitting in stillness for a few minutes and breathing the following prayer with the rhythm of your own breath:

(Inhaling) *Holy Spirit,* (exhaling) *let Your creative love move in me.*

Ponder Scripture

The earth was formless and empty, darkness was over the surface of the deep, and the Spirit of God was hovering over the waters.

— GENESIS 1:2

From the very beginning, the Holy Spirit was involved in creation, in the mystery of bringing beauty out of formlessness or emptiness. Picture Him hovering over your journey before you were even formed. Psalm 139:13 and 15 in *The Message* says, "Oh yes, you shaped me first inside, then out; you formed me in my mother's womb" and "You know exactly how I was made, bit by bit, how I was sculpted from nothing into something."

What happens in your heart when you think about the Spirit of God creatively hovering over you before you were even born?

Please read John 3:1-8, John 1:12-13, John 3:16, 2 Corinthians 5:17, Ezekiel 36:26, and Romans 5:5. After reading these verses, try to piece together the elements of your new birth. List your insights into why you were conceived, by whom, your actual new birth, and the Spirit's creative love in the process.

That moment when you were reborn, the Holy Spirit not only hovered and swirled around you, He began an intimate indwelling, a continual force making you radiant from the inside out. And that intimacy doesn't stop at your skin. The Holy Spirit draws threads of intimacy with the Father, with Jesus, with Himself and pulls them through us and uses them to bring community and connection with other believers.

The Holy Spirit brought the gift of creative participation to the artisans constructing the sanctuary (see Exodus 35:30–36:1). Today, the Holy Spirit gifts each child of God with a part in building up the body of Christ. We are all included in the creating of this beautiful mosaic of community in Christ. Every piece matters.

Please read Romans 12:6-8; 1 Corinthians 12:4-11; and Ephesians 4:11-13,16.

Go back over each passage and make a list of the gifts. You can simply list them here, draw symbols for each, or create a mosaic of the gifts.

At times, there is a hint of fear that lurks behind discovery of our gifts. We fear we will be the one exception to God's giving heart and come away empty-handed. We wonder how or if our lives will change. We fear that our gifts will represent something we really don't like or something that makes us want to hide. We wonder, *What if He asks me to do something outrageous?* We might even think that if we are unaware of our gifts, we won't be responsible to respond.

Sandi's Story

Sandi knew most of the information given out at church about God being a loving God, but that's exactly what it was: information. She struggled to know His generous love in her heart. She felt delight and surprise when she began to unwrap her gifts. They fit her. It was like she'd gone to a seamstress, been measured, and had a gown made to fit. The Spirit who hovered over the waters at creation, who sculpted her, who ushered in her new life in Christ, knew exactly how to outfit her heart. This was not to say she never again experienced discomfort at the prospect of using those gifts. Each time Sandi stepped out in faith, her physical heart might have been pounding at first but then gave way to the peace that comes from living from the core of who she was made to be. What was once an intimidating exploration of gifts became an intimate expression of her relationship with the indwelling Spirit.

Is there any way in which you've experienced reluctance to discover your gifts?

Have you taken a gift inventory, participated in a class exploring spiritual gifts, or in some other way asked the Holy Spirit to reveal your gifting? If so, what did you discover?

If not, would you consider investigating this topic further? If you do not know where to begin, ask a trusted pastor or friend for help or examine the resources available online. Willow Creek Church and Saddleback Church have both published gift inventories that you could access or order online.

Manifested Intimacy

Read 1 Corinthians 12:7 once again. *The Message* phrases it like this: "Each person is given something to do that shows who God is."

In the *Amplified Bible,* the wording is, "To each one is given the manifestation of the [Holy] Spirit [the evidence, the spiritual illumination of the Spirit] for good and profit."

Personalize this verse, reading it aloud with your name in the blank:

To _____ is given the manifestation of the [Holy] Spirit [the evidence, the spiritual illumination of the Spirit] for good and profit.

You and I are given revelation of the Spirit that demonstrates His heart to others and becomes part of who we are. In the deepest recesses of our innermost being, He discloses Himself. As we exercise the gifts He imparts, we reveal the Holy Spirit of almighty God. We radiate life. Like the motion of riding a bike or playing a piano, the movement becomes ingrained, one with our bodies.

Sometimes artists choose to manifest their hearts with living art, such as a living nativity, a drama, dance, or the 2008 Olympics opening ceremony in Beijing. In a sense, we are the canvas, the medium on and in which the Holy Spirit displays His creative love. I can't imagine anything more intimate. We radiate Him through the motion of His life lived out through us. Author David Benner wrote,

> Any authentic spiritual journey must grow from direct personal experience of God. There is no substitute for a genuine encounter with Perfect Love. "Knowledge by acquaintance," Tozer affirms, "is always better than mere knowledge by description."[1]

The more we express Him, the more we know Him.

In what ways are you becoming more intimately acquainted with Him as He sculpts you, His living work of art?

Glance back at 1 Corinthians 12, Romans 12, and Ephesians 4. Note that each passage leads to or ends with the proclamation that love is the substance that effectively saturates and invigorates the gifts. Love is the sparkling water that the gifts spring from and the channel they flow through. As the Spirit manifest Himself in and through us, love flows, creating community and leaving a trail of life and intimacy wherever it flows.

With that in mind, turn to Ezekiel 47:9-12 and draw (stick figures and basic shapes are fine) the vision described.

Spa Treatment

While on board a cruise ship, I scoped out the spa services. Appointments are available for most of what you can imagine and much of what you couldn't dream up. Encouraged by my husband to go ahead and indulge, I scheduled an aromatic lime ginger body scrub. The technician exfoliates the skin, sloughing off dead skin cells and then applies soothing moisture to reveal the radiance beneath the surface. The process is a little embarrassing if, like me, you're shy about revealing all your imperfections, cellulite, and so on. But it was incredibly relaxing and my skin did glow afterward, at least for a little while.

Sometimes we need regular spa breaks. Stress takes its toll and suppresses inner radiance. It hampers the creative love flowing in and through us. We might need a spiritual time of exfoliation to restore the sparkle.

What tends to hide or hinder the radiance of God in your life?

Will you go to the Spirit and ask Him to slough off old cells and recreate radiance in you?

Ongoing stress and exposure to harsh elements can also wear us down mentally. Sometimes it's as if we take our hearts and minds down smoggy streets, not realizing how much is seeping in and dulling our spirits. Try steeping your mind and emotions in Philippians 4:4-11 and Romans 8:6. How could anxiety block the Spirit's illumination?

How are you personally affected by what your mind dwells on?

How does your thinking affect your emotions?

Where do you think the shaping activity of the Spirit soaks through and brings life? Brainstorm some possible treatments for anxiousness and negative thinking based on Philippians 4:4-11 and Romans 8:6.

Consider trying one of these exercises this week:

- Fast from watching the news and reading the paper for a day or even a few days. Jot down any impact this has on your thinking.
- Work on memorizing Philippians 4:4-11. Write it down on a Post-it note or index card and carry it with you, repeating phrases and sentences until they become ingrained in your long-term memory. Ask the Holy Spirit to enable you to absorb these words and let them shape you.
- Meditate on Philippians 4:4-11, dwelling on a different phrase each day.

Reflect

I appeal to you therefore, brethren, and beg of you in view of [all] the mercies of God, to make a decisive dedication of your bodies [presenting all your members and faculties] as a living sacrifice, holy (devoted, consecrated) and well pleasing to God, which is your reasonable (rational, intelligent) service and spiritual worship.

— ROMANS 12:1, AMP

I love to watch sculptors at work whenever I have the opportunity. I've seen huge blocks of sand transformed into a scene I never thought could emerge from grains of sand. At a wood-carving contest, chunks of wood were shaped via chainsaws into bears, dragons, pumpkins, turtles, and so much more. Blocks of ice become intricate swans, or a hunk of clay an eagle. I look on amazed. Who would have thought all that was living beneath the surface?

With Romans 12:1 fresh in your mind, imagine you are a block of sand or ice, a chunk of wood, or a hunk of clay and the creative Spirit of God is hovering over you and flowing through you.

Which of these describes that thought?

- ◆ Scary
- ◆ Freeing
- ◆ Painful
- ◆ Hopeful
- ◆ Exciting
- ◆ Other _____

Lay yourself before God and allow Him to shape you and transform you into a radiant work of art that manifests His presence. What tools does He use? His hands, light, rushing water, soaking agents? What might the Holy Spirit be creating in you during this season of your life? What might the Holy Spirit be revealing in you and unveiling to the world? Write or draw any insights.

Respond

The Holy Spirit doesn't coerce you into becoming one who is radiant, one who more and more manifests the outpoured life of God. You have a choice to become a masterpiece. Though author Gordon MacKenzie's words were to artists, I think what he said can also apply to submitting our hearts to the creative force of love. He wrote,

You have a masterpiece inside you, too, you know. One unlike any that has ever been created, or ever will be. And remember: if you go to your grave without painting your masterpiece, it will not get painted. No one else can paint it. *Only you.*[2]

Mull over his words. Are there ways you can cooperate in the work of the Spirit this week as He unveils you, His masterpiece?

End this week by praying or singing (if you know the tune) the words of this old hymn as an offering to the Spirit of God of all you are and will become:

Take my life and let it be consecrated, Lord, to thee;
Take my moments and my days, let them flow in ceaseless praise;
Let them flow in ceaseless praise.
Take myself and I will be ever, only, all for thee.
Take my hands and let them move at the impulse of thy love;
At the impulse of thy love.
Take my feet and let them be swift and beautiful for thee.
Take myself and I will be ever, only, all for thee;
Ever, only, all for thee.
Take my voice and let me sing ever, only, for my King.
Take my lips and let them be filled with messages from thee;
Filled with messages from thee.
Take myself and I will be ever, only, all for thee.
Take my silver and my gold, not a mite would I withhold;

Not a mite would I withhold.
Take my intellect and use ev'ry pow'r as thou shalt choose.
Take myself and I will be ever, only, all for thee;
Ever, only, all for thee.
Take my will and make it thine, it shall be no longer mine.
Take my heart it is thine own, it shall be thy royal throne;
It shall be thy royal throne.
Take my love, my Lord, I pour at thy feet my treasure store;
Take myself and I will be ever, only, all for thee.
Ever, only, all for thee.[3]

Cleansing Streams

Come near to God and he will come near to you.
— JAMES 4:8

It's amazing how knowing we are deeply loved gives courage to let healing begin. Have you ever watched a little boy who discovers a splinter in his pinky finger and runs to Mommy with his "owie"? Maybe he wiggles, doesn't want to look at it, or resists having it removed. Yet his mom holds him in her lap as she gently does whatever is necessary to remove the splinter and bring relief. It still may hurt, but somehow the holding and snuggling ease the pain. Quiet words, a touch on the shoulder, a hug, or simply knowing we will never be left alone seem almost magical sometimes.

In preparation for receiving the healing and cleansing touch of the Spirit this week, come near to the heart of God and let the knowledge that you are welcomed and loved wash over you. Find a comfortable or cherished place to settle into and rest quietly there in the presence of God. Take some time to simply breathe. If you wish, hum or sing your favorite worship song. As you make yourself at home in His presence, invite the Holy Spirit to enfold you. Then lean in and whisper, "Come, Holy Spirit." Stay where you are for a few minutes, allowing Him to hold you. Jot down anything that describes how it feels to be near the Spirit of God.

As you dip your heart into cleansing waters this week, ask the Holy Spirit to keep you close, to cradle you. In the midst of the challenges and joys, turn into, not away from, Him and beseech Him to keep you near. David Benner called this "snuggling" with God. He wrote, "For love to transform us not only must we meet in vulnerability, we must also linger long enough for it to penetrate our woundedness. Snuggling keeps us in contact with love long enough that it has that effect."[1]

Consider sketching a symbol or picture as simple or elaborate as you wish that illustrates Benner's words.

Ponder Scripture

Over the years, many women have shared their fear of vulnerability or admitting imperfection. Some relate memories of feeling raked over the coals by their parents for failures, perceived or real. The response to a wrong was harsh, loud or deathly quiet, and brutal. There were assault words launched, such as "I knew you'd never amount to anything" or "Get out of here—I don't want to see your ugly face." Sometimes any glimmer of badness brought physical punishment.

Others experienced a more subtle form of rejection, but the message was conveyed that they were loved only when they were perfect. They learned to hide any failure, to try to cover up their struggles.

What has been your previous experience with admitting failure or being confronted with a wrong? Is there any sense in which you feel a need to hide all the bad stuff from God?

Can we trust the truth of our hearts to the searching and cleansing Spirit of God? One way of answering this question is to explore the atmosphere He provides for cleansing. Please read the following scriptures and record the heart of God toward you when you come to Him just as you are in honesty and humility.

- ◆   Psalm 103:8-14

- ◆   Isaiah 42:3

◆   Lamentations 3:22-23

◆   Joel 2:13

◆   Micah 7:18

◆   Luke 18:13-14

◆   Ephesians 2:4-5

◆   Hebrews 4:14-16

If you could give the cleansing waters a title based on these passages, what might it be?

With your title simmering on the back burner of your mind, will you trust your merciful God with any apprehension and fling your heart wide open to the searching of the Spirit?

Searching Words

I had very little comprehension of Christianity until my late twenties when I became a believer. But at around age twelve, I did experience brief intermittent bouts of exposure to one strain of religion. What I watched and heard was called being "under conviction." The people involved were supposed to wail and cry and be very, very sorry for their sins. They were to repent loudly and confess all their sins, and then, if they did this long enough and well enough, God might save them. There seemed to always be someone there questioning the sincerity and depths of the sorrow of the repentee and pronouncing the need for more wailing. I never understood what would constitute enough sorrow and confession.

For a while, I was terrified of what became to me three very scary words: *conviction*, *repentance*, and *confession*. Later, as an excited new Christian, I had to "rebrand" those words and give them access to my life. I've even come to a place of gratitude for one of the lessons of that time: Sin is grievous and destructive; it flies in the face of all that defines the holy beauty and love of God.

What do the words *conviction*, *repentance*, and *confession* stir up in you? Have they been ambiguous, frightening words to avoid or something else?

As we continue, I pray you will embark on a discovery of the intense love of the Holy Spirit, made evident through His convicting of hearts and His intertwining of repentance and confession to create transformed, free lives. Find a dictionary and look up the verb *convict*. Jot down a couple of words or phrases that help you understand this word.

Now turn to John 16:7-11. Consider what Jesus said about the activity of the Holy Spirit here. He pierces through the babble, surrounding us and making our need of Jesus clear. He spots and reveals any unbelief. He makes clear what it means to live in holiness and purity like Jesus and demonstrates Satan's condemnation and defeat.

Read Psalms 40:12 and 38:4. Do these verses lend any clarity to the idea of feeling conviction? If so, in what way?

Usually the conviction of the Spirit seems inconvenient and it's often painful, but it is interference with a purpose. It's about highlighting areas of our hearts that block the living flow of the Spirit. In John 7:38, Jesus said, "Whoever believes in me, as the Scripture has said, streams of living water will flow from within him." Unbelief, then, is one thing that we know blocks life. It's like the dead zone of cell phone commercials.

We might be at a place on our journey where we know we've

believed the gospel message but need that belief to characterize our daily life. Are there corners of unbelief in your heart that disrupt the flow of living water?

Beth Moore wrote,

> God wields incomparably great power for those who choose to believe. . . . More than enough to break the yoke of any bondage. Our belief unclogs the pipe and invites the power to flow. . . . Believe Him . . . and when you don't, cry out earnestly, "Help me overcome my unbelief!"[2]

If you are struggling with believing God in some way, try making the following prayer your own every day this week:

> Lord in Heaven, in every faith walk I encounter, keep working with me until You can victoriously boast, "You believe at last!" (John 16:31).[3]

Kind Piercings

Romans 2:4 assures us that it's the kindness of God that leads us to repentance. Although it can be hard to see it that way, the piercing of our hearts is a kindness of the Holy Spirit. Through His work, we can see the dead zones and embrace life instead. However, the Spirit does not force life down our throats. When our hearts are laid bare, we're presented with a life-or-death choice. We can choose to heed the voice of the Spirit or reject it. The apostle Paul wrote, "Do not grieve the Holy Spirit of God [do not offend or vex or sadden Him], by Whom you were sealed (marked, branded as God's own, secured) for the day of redemption" (Ephesians 4:30, AMP). "Do not quench (suppress or subdue) the [Holy] Spirit" (1 Thessalonians 5:19, AMP).

What might it look like to grieve, vex, quench, or suppress the Holy Spirit of God?

On the other hand, we can choose life. At times, it's as if the Spirit works to create willing hearts, to help us choose life when we let Him into our struggles. Then our eyes open and we begin to see the ugly reality of sin. Rather than turning a deaf ear, we turn toward the voice of the Spirit; we repent. Author Kathleen Norris told the story of a boy's poem titled "The Monster Who Was Sorry":

He began by admitting that he hates it when his father yells at him; his response in the poem is to throw his sister down the stairs, and then to wreck his room, and finally to wreck the whole town. The poem concludes: "Then I sit in my messy house and say to myself, 'I shouldn't have done all that.'" . . . The boy made a metaphor for himself that admitted the depth of his rage and gave him a way out. If that boy had been a novice in the fourth-century monastic desert, his elders might have told him that he was well on his way to repentance. . . . If the house is messy, they might have said, why not clean it up, why not make it into a place where God might wish to dwell?[4]

Describe a time when you felt a little like this boy.

In what places is the Holy Spirit inviting a cleanup effort?

Read James 4:7-10 as part of the cleanup process. Which words require action on your part? What does it say that God will do?

It's comforting to know we can draw near to God and hold on even as we survey the wake of destruction left by our sin. Nothing is unaffected. Our relationships with God, others, ourselves are sullied. But in the midst of the pain, there's hope.

Some time ago, I went into a surgery concerned about the pain that would follow. My brother, in his attempt to encourage me, said, "But, Rita, it will be a good pain." I wanted to throw something at him, but he was right. Recovery ultimately led to restoration.

What is your response to the idea of "good pain"?

Write any way in which the Spirit is speaking to your heart through the words of James 4.

Reflect

There's a fountain in my home that I love. I enjoy the sound of the water, the beauty the paths each stream of water makes down the rough surface, and the bubbling water over the river rocks. Lately the sound has been muted and much of the fountain is dry. For the complete flow to be restored, I need to wash away crusty blockages and remove the buildup of residue I didn't even know was there.

Our hearts need a thorough cleaning periodically too. Over the years, believers have used different methods to submit themselves to the cleansing streams of life. Twelve-step programs include a "searching and fearless moral inventory."[5] Some use the Ten Commandments or the seven deadly sins as measurement tools for their inventory. Martin Luther also recommended this, saying, "There is no better mirror in which to see your need than the Ten Commandments."[6] You may wish to turn to the commandments (see Exodus 20:1-21) and use them for a guideline or to participate in another way of taking inventory that will follow.

In either case, begin your time with this prayer from the book of Psalms:

Investigate my life, O God,
    find out everything about me;
Cross-examine and test me,
    get a clear picture of what I'm about;
See for yourself whether I've done anything wrong—
    then guide me on the road to eternal life. (139:23-24, MSG)

Which phrase of this prayer most causes you to tremble?

Pause for a moment and think back to the very beginning of this week's study. Check your position. Are you still snuggling?

Stay nestled in His arms and breathe deeply. Notice the fragrance of the waters and ask the Spirit for the courage to step into the cleansing waters. They are swirling with mercy, grace, and unconditional love.

Read aloud Galatians 5:16-26. Focus on the fruit of the Spirit in verses 22-23 and complete the following inventory. Score yourself by marking approximately where you fall on each continuum this week.

I stay in step with the Spirit expressing **love** in and through my daily life.

Rarely   Occasionally   Sometimes   Frequently

I stay in step with the Spirit expressing **joy** in and through my daily life.

Rarely   Occasionally   Sometimes   Frequently

I stay in step with the Spirit expressing **peace** in and through my daily life.

Rarely   Occasionally   Sometimes   Frequently

I stay in step with the Spirit expressing **patience** in and through my daily life.

Rarely   Occasionally   Sometimes   Frequently

I stay in step with the Spirit expressing **kindness** in and through my daily life.

Rarely   Occasionally   Sometimes   Frequently

I stay in step with the Spirit expressing **goodness** in and through my daily life.

_____

Rarely   Occasionally   Sometimes   Frequently

I stay in step with the Spirit expressing **faithfulness** in and through my daily life.

_____

Rarely   Occasionally   Sometimes   Frequently

I stay in step with the Spirit expressing **gentleness** in and through my daily life.

_____

Rarely   Occasionally   Sometimes   Frequently

I stay in step with the Spirit expressing **self-control** in and through my daily life.

_____

Rarely   Occasionally   Sometimes   Frequently

Choose one or two areas to focus on, becoming specific with your confession and need by filling in this sentence in whatever way best fits your journey right now:

I confess my lack of [a specific fruit] _____
as evidenced by _____.

Now using the information gleaned, pray Psalm 51, inserting specifics whenever possible and keeping in mind there is cleansing available because of the blood of Jesus.

Stay close, allowing the Spirit to soothe you. Feel the cleansing waters flow over every raw wounded area. Sit with open hands and imagine forgiveness poured over you. Receive it; rest in it.

Speak to your heart the words from these passages:

The sacrifices of God are a broken spirit;
    a broken and contrite heart,
    O God, you will not despise. (Psalm 51:17)

If we confess our sins, he is faithful and just and will forgive us
our sins and purify us from all unrighteousness. (1 John 1:9)

The process of highlighting brokenness is an activity born of love. The Spirit works to induce transformation, to birth newness of life from the inside out. Because you live by the Spirit, ask Him to keep you in step with Him more and more (see Galatians 5:25).

Staying in step might include acting on James 5:16, which exhorts, "Confess your sins to each other and pray for each other so that you may be healed. The prayer of a righteous man is powerful and effective." Think of someone you could invite into your journey and with whom you could pray. Although it might be scary, share a specific need for spiritual growth with that person and ask for prayer. If it seems no one is available for that kind of sharing, go to the Holy Spirit and ask Him to bring a prayer partner who will treat your heart with care.

Respond

Celebrate the wonder of living close to the Spirit; splash in the joy of the fresh life He brings to your heart. Read the following psalm in gratitude to God:

Count yourself lucky, how happy you must be—
>   you get a fresh start,
>   your slate's wiped clean.

Count yourself lucky—
>   GOD holds nothing against you
>   and you're holding nothing back from him.

When I kept it all inside,
>   my bones turned to powder,
>   my words became daylong groans.

The pressure never let up;
>   all the juices of my life dried up.

Then I let it all out;
>   I said, "I'll make a clean breast of my failures to GOD."

Suddenly the pressure was gone—
>   my guilt dissolved,
>   my sin disappeared.

These things add up. Every one of us needs to pray;
>   when all hell breaks loose and the dam bursts
>   we'll be on high ground, untouched.

GOD's my island hideaway,
>   keeps danger far from the shore,
>   throws garlands of hosannas around my neck. . . .

Celebrate GOD.
>   Sing together—everyone!
>   All you honest hearts, raise the roof! (Psalm 32:1-7,11, MSG)

Find one way you can raise the roof in celebration. You could:

- Twirl around
- Dance in the rain
- Take a symbolic shower
- Sing your heart out
- Go out for dinner
- Other _____

Whatever you choose to do, enter in with your whole heart and keep snuggling.

Please pray with me and continue to pray as you feel led:

> *Lord, I'm so amazed by Your mercy and grace. Thank You for sending Your Spirit to lead me to the throne of grace. Thank You for holding me even when I'm not all that embraceable. Thank You for seeing me through eyes of love. It feels wonderful to be clean, to know that You will never give up on me. Let the fruit of Your Spirit multiply in my life and transform me. How I love You. Be glorified in my life.*

A Warm Bath

When I was a girl, there were times life seemed cold, like frigid air seeping into my bones. I used to sit over the heater vent, trapping the warm air with a blanket. I would grab a good story and snuggle down into an imaginary world full of colorful characters. I wanted the physical coziness to warm me when I couldn't get warm inside. I'd stay there for hours and sometimes fall asleep. I never dreamed it possible to know that kind of warmth on the inside.

Think back over any memories that remind you of comfort or warmth. What textures, colors, scents, places, and people do you associate with those memories? Briefly describe a time you felt comforted.

Have you ever wondered what exactly it is that imparts comfort? I have. The mystery of it all draws me in, yet I cannot grasp it with any firmness. I have, at times, known a stilling of anxious clatter as I experienced what seemed to be the Spirit of God gripping my heart, like a hand reaching in and holding me still, keeping me whole. That kind of comfort escapes my ability to control or explain, yet it's as real as any tangible object my fingers grasp.

How might it feel to you to experience comfort in a sacred space deep within? Frederick Buechner suggested,

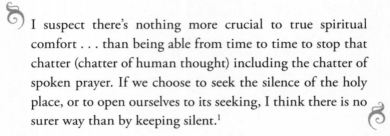

> I suspect there's nothing more crucial to true spiritual comfort . . . than being able from time to time to stop that chatter (chatter of human thought) including the chatter of spoken prayer. If we choose to seek the silence of the holy place, or to open ourselves to its seeking, I think there is no surer way than by keeping silent.[1]

Bask, as if in a warm bath, in Spirit-enfolded silence for a few minutes. Jot down any thoughts and ask the Holy Spirit to empower you to carry that sacred silence with you as you open the Word of God.

Ponder Scripture

John 14:18 assures us we are not left as orphans. Still, some of us live with scars of abandonment that get in the way of embracing that truth. Listen to the hearts of the women in the following stories.

Brittany's Story

Brittany finds herself doing and saying whatever she thinks is necessary to avoid abandonment. She senses this driving force propelling her to never be alone, to always have someone she can say she belongs to. Sometimes she's been chameleon-like, doing most anything and everything to keep a man around and losing much of herself in the process. She describes it as this need to fit in with someone, to be welcomed, and to know she belongs.

Anna's Story

Anna agrees with Brittany but adds that she feels caught in a vicious cycle. She is incredibly lonely and sleeps with guys in an attempt to manufacture physical comfort and the feeling she's not alone. The problem is that the relief is fleeting and often nonexistent. In her core, she still feels unknown and isolated.

Becca's Story

Becca isn't filling the holes in her spirit with sex or anything tangible. She shares that instead she finds herself agreeing with others, ordering what they order at a restaurant, copying likes and dislikes. Becca fears rejection and is hesitant to reveal herself. She longs for comforting relationships but is selective with where she'll let others in.

In what ways do you identify with the struggles of these women? Describe any way or time you've felt orphaned by anyone.

Comforting Presence

Parakletos is the word used in John 14:16 for the Holy Spirit. Over the years, *parakletos* has been translated Counselor, Comforter, Advocate,

Helper, Strengthener, and Standby.[2] In *The Message* translation of the Bible, the word is rendered "Friend." The *parakeltos* "does not merely put in a good word, but brings active help. The sense of helper and intercessor is suitable in all occurrences of the word."[3]

Which of those descriptors appeals most to your heart right now?

Why do you think this word stands out for you over the others?

Please read John 14:16-20,26-27. What does it mean to you today that the Spirit dwells in you and is with you forever?

In His tender goodness, God knew our need of knowing we belong to Him, now and eternally. One role of the Spirit is to incarnate that truth in our hearts. He marks us as His own. The life of the Spirit within us is real; it's dynamic and eternal. In many ways, He translates the heart of God to our hearts, making His transforming love known.

Meditate on the verses that follow, asking the Spirit to help you receive the comfort they offer:

> This resurrection life you received from God is not a timid, grave-tending life. It's adventurously expectant, greeting

God with a childlike "What's next, Papa?" God's Spirit touches our spirits and confirms who we really are. We know who he is, and we know who we are: Father and children. (Romans 8:15-16, MSG)

God affirms us, making us a sure thing in Christ, putting his Yes within us. By his Spirit he has stamped us with his eternal pledge—a sure beginning of what he is destined to complete. (2 Corinthians 1:22, MSG)

It's in Christ that you, once you heard the truth and believed it (this Message of your salvation), found yourselves home free—signed, sealed, and delivered by the Holy Spirit. This signet from God is the first installment on what's coming, a reminder that we'll get everything God has planned for us, a praising and glorious life. (Ephesians 1:13-14, MSG)

This is how we know we're living steadily and deeply in him, and he in us: He's given us life from his life, from his very own Spirit. (1 John 4:13, MSG)

How might you receive the comfort of God's Spirit touching your spirit?

Choose one or two of the four verses and form them into a prayer. Pray them to God, asking the Spirit to imprint them on your spirit, to drench you in the intimate warmth of His welcome. Pause for a few minutes and sit quietly or record your thoughts in your journal.

Comforting Hope

> *The word which God has written on the brow of every man is Hope.*
>
> — VICTOR HUGO

I've known the strange intermingling of ecstatic sunshiny moments and intense storms. At times, those moments seem to occur simultaneously and leave me feeling confused. Still, I know that rainy days mixed with sunshine can often produce rainbows. I've found myself praying, "Lord, help me see the rainbow."

Over the years, rainbows have become a symbol of hope. Read Genesis 9:12-17. What is it about rainbows that inspires hope?

In Romans 15:13, Paul wrote, "May the God of hope fill you with all joy and peace as you trust in him, so that you may overflow with hope by the power of the Holy Spirit." Picture an overflowing fountain. What would it be like to receive such an abundant outpouring of hope through the Holy Spirit?

John Ortberg suggested that we practice a form of measuring our personal hope supply. He said,

One indicator is how I face the morning. . . . There is a reason why the Scriptures say God's mercies are "new every morning." When I find myself waking up feeling overwhelmed by the tasks to be done during the day, I know hope is running low.[4]

Even if you aren't a morning person or need your cup of coffee first, try applying his hope screening system to your attitude toward facing a new day. How do you typically feel about the day as you wake up or once you are fully awake?

Maybe you're grappling with more than facing the morning; perhaps long before then, in the middle of the night, you're awakened with a sick feeling in the pit of your stomach. I battled with that enemy over the summer while my husband was hospitalized. I regularly woke up tormented with what was happening before my eyes and what could happen in the future. Dread crashed into illusions of control. I cried out, "Please, God, help me!" Often I turned on the light, sat up, and began receiving comfort and hope through Scripture. In those times, the Spirit reminded me who my hope was in and encouraged me to walk in hope rather than fear.

What encouragement can you take from the following passages of Scripture for yourself or maybe as a prayer for another? Jot down any words or phrases that remove fear and pour out hope.

- Psalm 33:18-22 _____
- Psalm 46 _____
- John 14:25-27 _____

Hold a troubling situation out to God. How can the intimacy of the indwelling Spirit help you take heart in the midst of trouble?

If you feel that your supply of hope is running low or has gone into hiding for a while, will you ask the Holy Spirit to help you take heart? Ask Him to penetrate every draining thought, feeling, and situation and rain down hope and life in, over, and through you. Go over these verses line by line and wait upon the Spirit:

> When life is heavy and hard to take,
>   go off by yourself. Enter the silence.
> Bow in prayer. Don't ask questions:
>   Wait for hope to appear. (Lamentations 3:28-29, MSG)

What might hope look like when it appears?

If most of life feels bright and friendly right now, celebrate. Enjoy this time and soak it in. Let it pool into a reservoir ready to be accessed when needed in your own life or in the life of another. Take a few minutes and write your prayers.

Comforting Encouragement

Heav'nly Spirit, gentle Spirit,
O descend on us, we pray;
Come console us and control us,
Christ most fair to us portray.
Come to cheer us, be thou near us,
Kindle in us heavn'ly love,
Keep us burning, humble, yearning,
Dwell in us, O heav'nly Dove.

— JOEL BLOMQUIST

Shadow was a puppy we brought home to the dismay of our cat, Hobo. The two were a long way from anything resembling friendship, but I was surprised by Hobo's merciful kitty heart. Shadow had just encountered his first veterinarian visit and experienced quite a bit of pain and terror with his first shots. As he lay on my lap producing the most pathetic-sounding cries, Hobo came and curled up next to him, comforting him with his warmth and presence. We sat that way for some time. I was too stunned to move.

A friend shared how she recently experienced a touch of comfort. She had just lived through one of the worst weeks of her life. She worked hard to muster up the courage to get through her days and to deal with family members who did not share her belief in God. A huge conflict swirled around the family, tainting every interaction. She attended a worship service and began weeping her way through a music-and-prayer time. A friend sitting nearby simply placed a hand over her hand, staying there until her tears began to dry up. The friend did not speak a single word, yet Becca felt the presence of God through that touch. Later, when she shared this story, she described that moment as one of the most comforting she'd ever experienced.

Have you ever experienced wordless comfort? Try expressing that comfort by marking on paper. You could use colors, shapes, stick figures, a sketch of hands, music notes, nature, rainbows, or even words.

When you long for comfort, turn to the Spirit. His presence, through someone else or not, is the one source of comfort that is full and real. Sometimes He uses physical touch alone; other times He includes words.

The apostle Paul experienced comfort and encouragement as the Holy Spirit moved through the life of another believer to come alongside him. As you read Acts 4:36-37; 9:26-27; 11:22-26,29-30, imagine you are putting together a profile of Barnabas. Try to include the following items and any others you would like to add:

- Original name
- Nickname
- Reason for nickname
- Source of strengths
- Specific actions
- Other _____

The encouragement flowing through Barnabas to Paul was Spirit-driven. In a sense, the Spirit gave Barnabas to Paul for a time. Henri Nouwen said, "Pain suffered alone feels very different from pain suffered alongside another. Even when the pain stays, we know how great the difference if another draws close, if another shares with us in it."[5]

Who has the Spirit given to you today or in the past? What do you learn about the Spirit through that gift? To whom have you been given?

When you are guided to comfort another, what do you learn about the Spirit as you participate in His work?

Reflect

Hope does not disappoint us, because God has poured out his love into our hearts by the Holy Spirit, whom he has given us.
— ROMANS 5:5

It might be helpful to physically touch and feel something you associate with comfort as you reflect on the comforting presence of the Spirit. Consider setting aside some time to try one or more of the following exercises:

- Prepare a warm drink in your favorite cup. Cradle the cup, inhale the aroma, relax, and swallow, savoring the taste as it slides all the way down. Imagine that the above-quoted scripture is like this cup. Hold it, notice every texture, take in the scent of hope, and then let it pour through you. What do you taste? How does it feel going down? Where is the moisture most needed?

- Plan time for a special bath. Write your favorite scripture from this week's study on an index card or something you can keep near you during your bath. Use your favorite scents; include the rituals and props that you find most relaxing. For example, light candles, play soft music, have a fresh drink available. Listen to the sounds as you draw your bath; watch the water give life to the bubbles. As you bathe, meditate on your chosen verse. Soak in it. Sink deeper into the water and ask the Spirit to saturate your heart with the words. Let an internal sense of comfort fuse with the physical warmth of the bath.

- Create a small soft material square (use whatever type of material you most enjoy). If you wish, stitch words of comfort or decorate the square. Keep it near your Bible and periodically take it out, running your fingers over the fabric and asking the Spirit to blanket your spirit with living warmth.

Respond

If you have gone a little way ahead of me, call back—
It will cheer my heart and help my feet along the stony track;
And if, perhaps, faith's light is dim, because the oil is low,
Your call will guide my lagging course as wearily I go.
Call back, and tell me that He went with you into the storm;
Call back, and say He kept you when the forest's roots were
*   torn;*
That, when the heavens thunder and the earthquake shook
*   the hill,*
He bore you up and held you where the lofty air was still.
*   — L. B. COWMAN, STREAMS IN THE DESERT*

Who has the Spirit placed in your life to "call back" to you in the last few weeks?

Think back over your walk with the Spirit. When have you felt His hand holding yours?

What comfort have you received as you journey with Him?

If you've kept a journal or written in the margins of your Bible, review some of those notes. How has He spoken living hope and encouragement over your life?

Take some time to note your responses as a way of "calling back" to yourself and as preparation to "call back" to others as the Spirit provides opportunity.

If possible, take a walk with the Spirit. Thank Him for His tender ministrations. Pour out your gratitude and then walk in the comforting silence of a love relationship that doesn't demand words.

Please pray with me and continue to pray as you feel led:

> *Holy Spirit, I cannot imagine walking through life without You. Thank You for the many times You have taken me by the hand. Thank You for holding me when I cry. Thank You for reassuring me and planting hope in my heart. When I feel alone, remind me of Your tender presence. I praise You. You are my true hope and comfort.*

Treasures of the Deep

As our family was taking a walk, I expressed delight at seeing a cactus common to our area growing near the path. My son, a young boy at that time, took that information and, to my surprise, came home one day and presented me with a similar cactus. In his eagerness to please me, he scraped and dug a cactus out of the ground with his bare hands and carried it home. I gasped when I saw his hands and worked to remove all the spines. That was a priceless gift—not the cactus itself but the tender heart of my son hoping to delight me.

What kind of treasures would you include in the "priceless" category?

As I prepared to write this week's study, I was struck by the incredible treasure we've been given as we relate intimately with the Spirit of God. He makes truth accessible to our hearts. In preparation for the opening of God's amazing Word, will you pray through the words of a beautiful hymn with me?

Open my eyes, that I may see
Glimpses of truth thou hast for me;
Place in my hands the wonderful key
That shall unclasp and set me free.
Silently now I wait for thee,
Ready my God, thy will to see;
Open my eyes, illumine me,
Spirit divine!

Open my ears, that I may hear
Voices of truth thou sendest clear;
And while the wave notes fall on my ear,
Everything false will disappear.
Silently now I wait for thee,
Ready my God, thy will to see;
Open my ears, illumine me,
Spirit divine![1]

Ponder Scripture

Please read John 16:12-15 a few times, letting the words swirl around in your mind. Then try to write your own paraphrase of the verses.

The Spirit glorifies Jesus, taking what is His and helping us to see it, to know in a way that surpasses simple accumulation of knowledge.

How has the Spirit revealed to you the heart of God in the past few days?

The Holy Spirit deepens our knowing of Jesus. He brings the treasure of intimate connection to life. Go over the words of Ephesians 1:17-19 with an open and prayerful heart. Think of the ways you've grown to know Jesus and what you know about Him. Make a list of some of your favorite things about Jesus.

In what area would you like your knowledge (not just facts but internal knowing) of God to grow?

With that in mind, pray through the Ephesians passage more specifically.

Digging for Treasure

Turn to 1 Corinthians 2:10-16 and read as if you are digging for treasure. What jewels do you find? What do you think differentiates the spirit of this world from the Spirit of God?

Those who do not know Jesus do not have the Spirit. They are left in the dark. Does that affect your level of compassion and concern and your attitude toward them? If so, in what ways?

Philosophy professor, speaker, and author Dallas Willard reminded us,

> When we constantly and thoughtfully engage with the ideas, images, and information that are provided by God through the Scriptures, his Son Jesus, and the lives and experiences of his people through the ages, we are nourished by the Holy Spirit in ways far beyond our own efforts or understanding. This transforms our entire life.[2]

We are not stuck out here on our own, orphaned, and chasing after life with distorted eyesight and hearing. Living within us is the very Spirit of God, the Spirit who knows God's thoughts, who "searches all things, even the deep things of God" (1 Corinthians 2:10). How does that truth affect you?

There are specific times I've needed an interpreter to translate the true meaning of another's words. The letters I receive from a child in a South American country are a great example. Without interpretation, I would be groping through the words, trying to lay hold of meaning. Before I receive the letters, a translator has already written out the message in a way I can understand.

The Holy Spirit interprets, translates, and helps us to take in the Word of God. He's never unsure of a meaning. In 1 Corinthians 2:13, Paul wrote, "We speak . . . in words taught by the Spirit, expressing spiritual truths in spiritual words." Another way of translating that last phrase is, "but in words taught by the Spirit, interpreting spiritual truths to spiritual men."

If you can, describe a time when the Spirit provided you with comprehension of vital truth.

Open Communion and Discernment

Moving on through the 1 Corinthians passage, we discover the treasure of spiritual discernment. I love the way *The Message* words verse 14: "Spirit can be known only by spirit—God's Spirit and our spirits in open communion." The Spirit doesn't offer just a sterile translation of words; it interprets the heart of God, bringing connection, creating open communion.

In what ways have you been drawn to or pushed away from the thought of open communion with the Spirit?

The expression of spiritual discernment as akin to open communion takes it beyond the level of an inanimate object. "Discernment . . . is the journey from spiritual blindness (not seeing God anywhere or seeing him only where we expect to see him) to spiritual sight (finding God everywhere, especially where we least expect it)."[3]

One of my favorite professors discussed discernment as a lifestyle. She spoke of discernment as the abundant way of life in the Spirit, "in which we are taught, led, comforted, and empowered."[4] That lifestyle takes us to new depths in relationship with God and with others. We become increasingly freed to connect honestly. Our fear of diving in might at times remain, but we're given courage to venture below the surface. In attitude, mannerisms, and habits of speech, we live in sync with the truth, with the guidance of our perfect Counselor. We listen to the promptings of the Spirit in our relationships, discerning his direction and being freed to go deeper in our communion with our God.[5]

Going Deeper

In Jan Karon's MITFORD novels, Fancy is a hairstylist whose endless chatter exhausts Father Tim. In the midst of one simple haircut, she covered all of these subjects: the barber's drinking habits, fur coats from yard sales, cold-weather predictions, chewing gum, diabetic diets, snake handling, dying the principal's hair, and more.[6]

When I read the stories, I laugh, but if I'm honest I have to admit that when I'm nervous, I can be prone to incessant chatter. Rather than pausing, asking the Spirit to pervade and invade the situation, I let anxiousness drive me to speak when I should be silent, talk about the weather when I could dive deeper, or dive deeper when I should wait.

When do you find it hard to practice a lifestyle of discernment as you connect with others?

I'm drawn to and pierced by Richard Foster's assessment: "Superficiality is the curse of our age. . . . The desperate need today is not for a greater number of intelligent people, or gifted people, but for deep people."[7]

Deep people aren't "microwaved" in a few minutes. It's time spent in that Spirit-to-spirit communion that erodes the tendency to live on or just below the surface. It's the internal abundance of the Spirit that fuels courageous connecting.

Lectio divina is a practice that can help us go deeper. It teaches us to attend to the Spirit as He interprets truth to our hearts. It helps us engage in Spirit-to-spirit communion. Jon Johnson wrote,

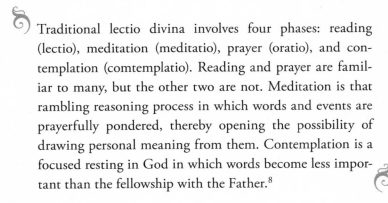

> Traditional lectio divina involves four phases: reading (lectio), meditation (meditatio), prayer (oratio), and con-templation (comtemplatio). Reading and prayer are famil-iar to many, but the other two are not. Meditation is that rambling reasoning process in which words and events are prayerfully pondered, thereby opening the possibility of drawing personal meaning from them. Contemplation is a focused resting in God in which words become less impor-tant than the fellowship with the Father.[8]

Our approach here won't necessarily be linear or formulaic, but I hope we can incorporate the basic concepts of *lectio* to explore a passage of Scripture and ask the Spirit to reveal Jesus to our hearts.

Before we dive into the passage, let your heart have a moment to become still. You might wish to repeat the following breath prayer a few times:

Holy Spirit (breathing in), *take me deeper* (breathing out).

Please turn to John 13:1-17. Take your time as your read each word out loud. As you chew on this passage, keep in mind a little background information:

- Just before this scene takes place, the disciples were arguing about who was the greatest.
- This section of Scripture is part of Jesus' last instructions to His disciples. He knows that events have been set in motion propelling Him toward the cross.[9]
- People wore open sandals on dusty roads, making regular foot washing essential. Typically this was a job that fell to the servants.[10]
- Judas is still present. Jesus knows that Judas will betray him, yet He washes his feet.

Read the passage again, silently this time. Jot down any words and phrases that seem to leap off the page at you.

Slowly go through the passage again, but as you read, imagine that you are there and Jesus is taking your bare foot in His hands. Wiggle your toes and feel the water on your feet. Feel the caress of the towel as Jesus dries your feet. Hear Him speaking the words of this passage to you. What are you thinking and feeling at this moment? How do you respond? Do you look down or into His eyes? Do you speak or stay silent?

Read over the passage aloud one more time. Silently reflect on or give yourself permission to wonder about the following questions: What is the Spirit revealing about Jesus to you? What is the Spirit revealing about you?

Think about and write down any way in which you can carry this communion with the Spirit into the rest of your day or week.

Reflect

I am fascinated with the beautiful world under the Caribbean Ocean. I've had opportunity to drift along off the coast of Curacao in a glass-bottom boat and to snorkel near Barbados. The rich colors, breathtaking coral, marine life, and even the sparkling white sand are stunning. On one particular excursion, we were able to shoot a number of pictures. Today I look at them and remember. They are evidence of a time that seems to quickly dissolve in the face of daily life. The images remind me that what I saw under the surface of those mysterious waters was real. They lure me back in thought to those places, and I'm captured anew by the wonders of the deep.

Spend some time reflecting on an excursion you've taken with the

Spirit into the "deep things of God" (1 Corinthians 2:10). Maybe it was in a particular passage of the Bible, a message you heard, a song that drew you in. Walk back through the details. What did you feel, see, and hear?

As you reflect, you might wish to explore one or both of the following exercises:

1. Make an entry in your journal similar to a diver's log. Record the details of your excursion: the how, what, where, when, and why.

2. Try to picture an object or image that symbolizes:

- ♦ The impact on your heart
- ♦ A new freedom
- ♦ Developing discernment
- ♦ Open communion
- ♦ New truths learned
- ♦ Other _____

Take some photographs of your symbolic image and place them in a journal, scrapbook, or photo album. Label each one and allow them to lure you back to the deep, to the encompassing waters of Spirit-to-spirit communion.

Respond

Write my words on your heart and meditate diligently on them, for in the time of temptation they will be very necessary for you. What you do not understand as you read you will understand in the day of visitation.

— THOMAS À KEMPIS

If I had to find one word to describe how belief came to take hold of me, it would be repetition.

— KATHLEEN NORRIS

As we take truth into our hearts and give it access to the inner workings of our lives, we are transformed. We become a treasure chest, holding and displaying the beauty and glory of the Lord. One method of honoring and cherishing what we've been given is committing to memory words of Scripture imprinted on our spirit. Even if your first thought is *But I can't even remember where I left my keys*, consider simply engaging in the process. As you do, you might or might not be able to recite every word from memory, but as you review and reflect and pray, the truth of the words will become part of your being.

Choose a verse, verses, or even a phrase that caught your attention this week and write it here along with the reference information.

Read it aloud. Next, write it out somewhere that it will be easy to access and see often, perhaps on an index card or in your weekly planner. Then pray through the words, asking the Spirit to bring them to life. Soak your heart in the passage until it becomes like a cherished image imprinted on your spirit.

Will you please pray along with me?

> *Living Spirit of God, thank You for holding on to me as You take me with You into the depths. I'm lost in wonder as You reveal riches, and I tremble with anticipation at the thought of what I have yet to encounter. Transform me as we go. Store in my heart the riches of Scripture; create in me a living treasure chest. Unveil the glory of Jesus in me and through me. Be glorified in me. Keep me near, keep me diving deep, keep me seeking open communion. How I love and treasure You. Amen.*

Powerful Waters

Searching for waterfalls has become one of my hobbies. I love the sight and sound of water cascading over rocks, dropping over dramatic cliffs, and spilling over tiers that nature staged just for it to touch. Niagara Falls is one of my favorites. The raw force and volume of the water inspires awe. On my last visit there, I took a guided tour on boardwalks that allowed me to experience the falls up close and personal. I inched my way as close as possible and stopped there, feeling small and weak yet somehow exhilarated. As the water sprayed my face, I marveled at the demonstration of sheer power pouring down. Everything the water touched was affected.

Standing there, it hit me: Impressive and majestic as the falls are, they only hint at the power of God. My heart in my throat, I worshipped God right there, knowing in a new way some of the truths on display in these passages:

> Mightier than the thunder of the great waters,
>   mightier than the breakers of the sea—
>   the LORD on high is mighty. (Psalm 93:4)

Ascribe to the LORD, O mighty ones,
　　ascribe to the LORD glory and strength.
Ascribe to the LORD the glory due his name;
　　worship the LORD in the splendor of his holiness.

The voice of the LORD is over the waters;
　　the God of glory thunders,
　　the LORD thunders over the mighty waters.
The voice of the LORD is powerful;
　　the voice of the LORD is majestic.
The voice of the LORD breaks the cedars;
　　the LORD breaks in pieces the cedars of Lebanon.
He makes Lebanon skip like a calf,
　　Sirion like a young wild ox.
The voice of the LORD strikes
　　with flashes of lightning.
The voice of the LORD shakes the desert;
　　the LORD shakes the Desert of Kadesh.
The voice of the LORD twists the oaks
　　and strips the forests bare.
And in his temple all cry, "Glory!"

The LORD sits enthroned over the flood;
　　the LORD is enthroned as King forever.
The LORD gives strength to his people;
　　the LORD blesses his people with peace. (Psalm 29)

The power of God is breathtaking. His power raised Jesus from the dead, calmed a storm with a word, changes stubborn hearts, creates from nothing, restrains wrath, and much, much more. His power can come with brute force or a gentle whisper. It's beyond my comprehension or ability to corral or contain. Yet, because the Spirit of God lives in me, I'm on intimate terms with power, a power that brings peace.

That seems almost surreal and leaves me on my knees. Will you worship with me?

Pause and adopt whatever posture best fits your spirit at this moment. Grant yourself a little time to contemplate the might and the intimacy of the Spirit of God. If you wish, write any impressions here.

Ponder Scripture

"You shall receive power when the Holy Spirit has come upon you" (Acts 1:8)—not power as a gift from the Holy Spirit; the power is the Holy Spirit, not something he gives us.

— OSWALD CHAMBERS

When the Holy Spirit came to live in our hearts, power came to live within. He's not a commodity or object that comes and goes; He is present but not coercive. We choose to either go with or block the flow. Oswald Chambers said, "Any effort to 'hang on' to the least bit of our own power will only diminish the life of Jesus in us. We have to keep letting go, and slowly, but surely, the great full life of God will invade us, penetrating every part."[1]

Read Ephesians 3:16-21, noting the effects of the Spirit's power. In what way do you think the ability to grasp love could be a power struggle? What obstacles block the ability to get a grip on the amazing love of Christ?

Madeleine L'Engle told a sad story of a father who must have known incredible hurt and betrayal. In his effort to protect his son,

he was emphatic in telling the little boy that *nobody* can be trusted. One evening when the father came home, his son came running down the stairs to greet him, and the father stopped him at the landing. "Son," he said, "Daddy has taught you that people are not to be trusted, hasn't he?" "Yes, Daddy." "You can't trust anybody, can you?" "No, Daddy." "But you can trust Daddy, can't you?" "Oh, yes, Daddy." The father then held out his arms and said, "Jump," and the little boy jumped with absolute trust that his father's arms were waiting or him. But the father stepped aside and let the little boy fall crashing to the floor. "You see," he said to his son, "you must trust *nobody*."[2]

What is your response to this story? Do you recognize any themes from your own life?

Though it might not have been deliberate, many of us have been taught never to trust anyone. We work hard to earn love, settle for illusions of love, or give up on ever knowing authentic love. The idea of letting go of our power, illusion or not, and allowing the power of the Spirit to take over is terrifying. We fear in letting go there will be nothing there, that we'll plummet and crash. But when we let the Spirit carry us, it's exhilarating, like a cushioned free fall. Through the Spirit at home in us, we really can rely on the spacious wonder of God's love.

What might get in your way of living in the middle of that love?

Bring those obstacles to the Spirit and ask Him to remove them so you can grasp the wonder of the love that lives in you and that you live in.

Prayerfully read over the following quote and let the Spirit pour over your heart the powerful, grace-filled love of Christ.

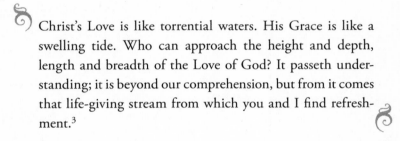

Christ's Love is like torrential waters. His Grace is like a swelling tide. Who can approach the height and depth, length and breadth of the Love of God? It passeth understanding; it is beyond our comprehension, but from it comes that life-giving stream from which you and I find refreshment.[3]

Think about the most grandiose, extravagant dimensions you can imagine and then fill in the following blanks:

Love longer than _____

Love wider than _____

Love higher than _____

Love deeper than _____

Picture yourself held, surrounded, enfolded in that kind of love. What does that feel like?

It's through the inner power of the Spirit that you begin to comprehend what you've been given and become a powerhouse of love. In the *Amplified Bible*, Ephesians 3:19 is worded,

> [That you may really come] to know [practically, through experience for yourselves] the love of Christ, which far surpasses mere knowledge [without experience]; that you may be filled [through all your being] unto all the fullness of God [may have the richest measure of the divine Presence, and become a body wholly filled and flooded with God Himself]!

What kind of freedom might you experience if you are flooded with God Himself? Try to name one aspect of your daily life that would be affected.

Prayer Flooded with the Life of God

Much of our journeys are laden with intangibles, the things we sense but have no idea how to articulate. Sorrows, temptations, confusion, and yearnings often defy expression. Tears might fall, but words, if they're present at all, seem stillborn. In those moments, a sense of powerlessness threatens to pervade our spirits. But the Spirit of God, like an unseen underwater current, connects us to the source of life.

Please look up and attend to the message of Romans 8:26-27. The Spirit knows the perfect will of God and knows our hearts better than we know them ourselves. He empowers us through intercessory prayer. He groans on our behalf.

What is created in you when you think of the Spirit feeling your need so deeply He groans? What situation, relationship, or personal challenge leaves you helpless, unsure how to pray?

Don't worry if there's a sense or impression you just can't label. For now, leave the struggle for words behind. Remind your heart of the dynamic love revealed to you by the Spirit. Know that He cares more than you can possibly imagine. Pretend you hold the named or unnamed challenge and simply extend your hands with the palms facing up. Ask the Spirit to intervene, to intercede perfectly and powerfully. Then turn your hands palm down; feel the release and let Him take over. When you are tempted to clutch at or fidget with the problem, physically stop in your tracks, turn your palms down, and ask the Spirit to help you let go and rest as often as necessary.

Go back to Romans 8:26-27 one more time. Linger over the words, asking the Spirit to make them real to your heart. In your journal write a thank-you note to the Holy Spirit that showers Him with gratitude for actively loving you in prayer.

Fullness of Love for Others

The intercession of the Holy Spirit is evidence of the extra-dimensional nature of the love living in us. That same love pushes past barriers to flow outward to others. As the Spirit pursues, draws, illumines, strengthens, and comforts, we are invited and empowered to participate. He can flow through us, prompting prayer in a myriad of ways. Consider the activity of the Holy Spirit in these stories:

- An urging took hold of me and I began to pray for my future grandchildren. Tears flowed as I poured out a desire for their care and protection. I prayed for them to ultimately come to know Jesus and become shining lights that others may know Him. Within a few months, I received a phone call from my son telling me his girlfriend was pregnant. The Holy Spirit allowed me to begin actively loving my granddaughter before I knew of her conception.
- A friend tells me of waking in the middle of the night from a sound sleep, not frazzled or reluctant but with dawning

purpose. Her mind is usually quite clear. She senses a nudge, a prodding to pray for a specific person or situation. Sometimes she hears absolutely nothing to confirm her nocturnal activity, but often she will become aware later of the reason behind the prompting to pray. She feels an awareness of the power of God working in her, including her in His work, and trembles in wonder.

◆ In a recent *Pray!* magazine article, Connie Willems told of her journey into listening prayer. She wrote,

> The people I was praying with *expected God to join us* and interact with us as we prayed. Instead of moving automatically from one request to another, we waited for God to show us what to pray about. For me that meant learning to listen to what others were praying and to what the Holy Spirit was whispering to me. . . . The expectation that God wanted to join us moved my experience of prayer beyond "right and good" to alive and enjoyable.[4]

◆ A small group united around the purpose of praying for those in their lives who did not yet know the Lord. The Spirit knit their hearts together with a yearning for others to know the amazing love they had received. One member chose at times to pray the words of Scripture back to the Lord. For example, she prayed for a specific person that the Lord would "open their eyes and turn them from darkness to light, and from the power of Satan to God, so that they may receive forgiveness of sins" (Acts 26:18).

◆ At one time, I worked for a ministry. In preparation for the day, I was routinely opening doors to the rooms. As I pushed one door open, I was transported from routine to holy ground. A noticeably frail elderly woman was kneeling on the hard floor with a stack of prayer requests before her. Alone in that room, she fervently lifted every person to the Lord with her whole being. I closed the door quickly, but that image of power and love synergistically at work stayed with me.

Which of these prayer stories draws you in today? Is there any way in which you sense encouragement, longing, and invitation?

Over the next week, experiment with one or more of the following ways of opening yourself to the Spirit and expressing the full love of the Lord in prayer:

- Ephesians 3:20 says, "Now to him who is able to do immeasurably more than all we ask or imagine, according to his power that is at work within us." Ask the Spirit to bring a person or situation to mind. Then simply pray, "Lord, please [in this person or situation] do beyond what I can ask or even imagine. Thank You for Your power at work [in this life or situation]." Then leave the prayer with the Lord.
- Invite the Holy Spirit to guide your time of prayer and let His love spill out. As a person or situation comes to mind, review the details, offering them to the Lord. Ask the Spirit to empower you to see as He sees, to feel His heart. Sit quietly. Listen and wait. As you sense the Spirit's guidance, pray.
- Open a notebook or journal and begin writing your prayer. Hold nothing back. Don't worry about punctuation or how it sounds or looks to others. This is between you and the Lord. It's okay if you are surprised at what comes pouring out. Know that He's not surprised.

◆ Let an ordinary week scroll through your mind and think of the people you interact with regularly. Who are the people in your world? Whose life touches yours and vice versa? Make a list of those people. Now lay your list before the Lord and pray, "Holy Spirit, I believe that You know every need, hurt, joy, and longing of each person on this list. I commit them all to You. Will You show me which of these people You intend for me to pray for regularly. I trust You to empower and lead those prayers. Thank You for flowing in me and through me, for making me one with You in the work of displaying the magnificent love of Christ to those around me. Amen." Brainstorm some ways you can remind yourself to lift that person to the Lord.

If appropriate, and without revealing specific confidence or protected information, share your experience in prayer with another.

Which one of these practices, if any, would you be most likely to repeat?

Spirit-Life Flowing Outward

What is the greatest crime in the desert? Finding water and keeping silent.

— ARAB PROVERB

Attend to the following Scripture passages, noticing any ways in which they intersect. It may be helpful to mark commonalities or list them in the margin as you go.

Jesus came to them said, "All authority in heaven and on earth has been given to me. Therefore go and make disciples of all nations, baptizing them in the name of the Father and of the Son and of the Holy Spirit, and teaching them to obey everything I have commanded you. And surely I am with you always, to the very end of the age." (Matthew 28:18-20)

I tell you the truth: It is for your good that I am going away. Unless I go away, the Counselor will not come to you; but if I go, I will send him to you. When he comes, he will convict the world of guilt in regard to sin and righteousness and judgment. (John 16:7-8)

You will receive power when the Holy Spirit comes on you; and you will be my witnesses in Jerusalem, and in all Judea and Samaria, and to the ends of the earth. (Acts 1:8)

Christ's love compels us, because we are convinced that one died for all, and therefore all died. (2 Corinthians 5:14)

We proclaim him, admonishing and teaching everyone with all wisdom, so that we may present everyone perfect in Christ. To this end I labor, struggling with all his energy, which so powerfully works in me. (Colossians 1:28-29)

Look back over each verse, asking yourself what you see as your role and God's role in living out these verses.

Scripture	God's Part	My Part
Matthew 28:18-20		
John 16:7-8		

Acts 1:8		
2 Corinthians 5:14		
Colossians 1:28-29		

How could living out these passages become an expression of indwelling multidimensional love?

Which of these describes the prospect of leaning into these verses?

- Scary
- Exciting
- Both scary and exciting
- Impossible
- Overwhelming
- Other _____

What would help you open yourself more to the Spirit as a vessel of power and love?

Reflect

To be a witness does not consist in engaging in propaganda, not even in stirring people up, but in being a living mystery. It means to live in such a way that one's life would not make sense if God did not exist.

— EMMANUEL CARDINAL SUHARD

Imagine for a moment that Oprah has invited you on her show to share a portion of your personal journey. You are given the primary interview questions to think over ahead of time. They are:

- When and why did you first invite Christ to dwell in your heart by faith?
- In what way has the Spirit empowered you to grasp the extravagant love of Jesus?
- How does your life showcase God's existence?

Take the time you need to entertain the questions and then give your answers. You might choose to express them in words, a painting, a dance, a song, or whatever way you wish to communicate your answers.

Ask the Holy Spirit to provide you with someone with whom you can share this exercise or pieces of this exercise. Let Him supply the power, courage, and love to show your heart to another.

Respond

Spend some time reveling in the wonder of the Spirit's indwelling. Rejoice in the intimacy of experiencing the Lord's powerful love in your innermost being. Celebrate Him through this psalm as if you were singing it at the top of your lungs:

> I lift you high in praise, my God, O my King!
>   and I'll bless your name into eternity.
> I'll bless you every day,
>   and keep it up from now to eternity.
> GOD is magnificent; he can never be praised enough.
>   There are no boundaries to his greatness.
> Generation after generation stands in awe of your work;
>   each one tells stories of your mighty acts.
> Your beauty and splendor have everyone talking;
>   I compose songs on your wonders
> Your marvelous doings are headline news;
>   I could write a book full of the details of your greatness.
> The fame of your goodness spreads across the country;
>   your righteousness is on everyone's lips.
> GOD is all mercy and grace—
>   not quick to anger, is rich in love.
> GOD is good to one and all;
>   everything he does is suffused with grace.
> Creation and creatures applaud you, GOD;
>   your holy people bless you.
> They talk about the glories of your rule,
>   they exclaim over your splendor,
> Letting the world know of your power for good,
>   the lavish splendor of your kingdom. . . .
> My mouth is filled with GOD's praise.
>   Let everything living bless him,
>   bless his holy name from now to eternity! (145:1-12,21, MSG)

Overflow of Life

As I write this, Thanksgiving is just around the corner. It's almost time to begin watching the many versions of *A Christmas Carol*. The story is my husband's favorite. Annually, we watch Scrooge's change of heart in *The Muppet Christmas Carol*, *Mister Magoo's Christmas Carol*, *Scrooged*, *Scrooge: The Musical*, *Ms. Scrooge*, and more.

One reason Dickens's story is so celebrated is the mirror it holds up for our hearts. At one time or another, we've all known the heartache of behaving like or relating to a Scrooge. Prior to his metamorphic night with the ghosts, fear and greed ravished him. In spite of his hoarding and accumulating of money, Scrooge was impoverished. It was about far more than seeing the glass half empty or half full; a dearth of inner life characterized his spirit. Then life fell down upon him and within him. He went forward materially and relationally with a rich heart. Do you ever wonder if Scrooge struggled weeks, months, or years later with letting his old self rule? He might have, but I like to hope the living waters still overflowed—that the inner heart with all the ups and downs of life still flourished.

As we begin to live out our status as new creations, as the river flows to the deepest recesses of our beings, we become people who live with an attitude of "abundance rather than scarcity."[1] Some days it's harder to trust the supply than others, but the water is plentiful. Some days relationships bear the marks of dryness and drought. Sometimes our behavior seems to slow the water down to a trickle or drip. Still, the abundance is there to access, to transform us and help us live closer to what and who we were made for.

When are you most tempted to see through the lens of scarcity? When is it easiest for you to see life from a perspective of abundance?

Pause and feel the pulsing waters moving in you. Invite the Spirit to drench you in the awareness of abundant life as you open the Word of God.

Ponder Scripture

They feast on the abundance of your house;
*   you give them drink from your river of delights.*
For with you is the fountain of life;
*   in your light we see light.*

— PSALM 36:8-9

As believers, we receive the promise of life through the Spirit. We enter into the beauty of prophecy fulfilled and yet to come, the eternal destiny that begins now for all who will receive. Once more, will you step with me into the unlimited supply of living water in Ezekiel 47:6-12? Immerse yourself in the images, noticing the overflow of life.

Focus on verse 12. Underline the words and phrases that shout abundance (*all, both,* and so on):

Fruit trees of all kinds will grow on both banks of the river. Their leaves will not wither, nor will their fruit fail. Every month they will bear, because the water from the sanctuary flows to them. Their fruit will serve for food and their leaves for healing.

The inexhaustible source of water is key for the fruit trees. Their root system has direct access to the river of life. They can't dredge it up on their own, manufacture it, or substitute anything else for it. Our spirits also need the dynamic water emanating from the sanctuary. Anything else is stagnant.

What sneaks in and tries to become a counterfeit life source for you? How might you stay open to the continuous stream of living water?

Paint in your mind a vivid picture of these magnificent fruit trees. Not only is the fruit full of life, so are the leaves. Imagine resting in the shade on a scorching day, letting coolness soothe your skin and restore sapped energy. Who have you known to be like a human version of these trees? Whose very presence provides shade for your weary soul? What about that person is sheltering?

Pause and write a prayer thanking God for that person and then asking the Spirit to allow you the privilege of becoming like a shade tree for another.

His Life Overflowing

Please turn to and read Galatians 5:16-26. *The Message* words verses 19-21 this way:

> It is obvious what kind of life develops out of trying to get your own way all the time: repetitive, loveless, cheap sex; a stinking accumulation of mental and emotional garbage; frenzied and joyless grabs for happiness; trinket gods; magic-show religion; paranoid loneliness; cutthroat competition; all-consuming-yet-never-satisfied wants; a brutal temper; an impotence to love or be loved; divided homes and divided lives; small-minded and lopsided pursuits; the vicious habit of depersonalizing everyone into a rival; uncontrolled and uncontrollable addictions; ugly parodies of community. I could go on.

What thoughts, emotions, and actions characterize a life that is not Spirit led?

What aspects of destruction listed in this passage stand out to you?

Read verses 22-26 again. When you think of keeping in step with someone, what does that look like?

The fruit of the Spirit isn't a wish list for Christian behavior; it's an expression of relationship and vital life-giving connection. It's evidence of intimacy that spurs transformation in the midst of bad-hair days, conflicts with family and friends, deep disappointment, suffering, lonely days, dealing with difficult people, and heartbreak.

One devotional put it this way:

> Behold, I have placed within you a spring of living water. For My Spirit shall be a continual flowing forth of life from your innermost being. . . . It is My Life I am giving you. It is not an emotion; it is not a virtue, though these may subsequently follow. It is Myself. Divine grace, heavenly love, infinite mercy, fathomless peace—all these will spring forth unbeckoned and irrepressible out of the depths within you because My Spirit has taken residence there.[2]

The Spirit-filled life is God's life expressed in and through us. It is not earned but is gifted to us by the Father (see Luke 11:13). We are given His peace, His joy, His love, His abundant life. Often we think of this list as ways we extend life to others, but it is also the life of the Spirit extended to us. Linger over Galatians 5:22-23. How has the fruit of the Spirit brought wholeness to your inner being?

Imagine you are creating or helping to film videos for an Internet site such as YouTube. Each video is designed to depict an aspect or aspects of the fruit of the Spirit. We'll look at a few scriptures and offer questions to get you thinking. Have fun designing some virtual videos on paper or listing ideas and thoughts to include under the "Video Notes" section.

Love

Agape, the word translated "love" in Galatians 5, goes beyond our usual concept of love. It's more than the "I want you" look in romantic comedies. Author Mark Buchanan suggested, "It exists free of conditions, fueled by something within itself rather than evoked by something outside itself. . . . It is *unprovoked love*."[3]

As you consider the following scriptures, note any descriptive words, phrases, and images that pop into your head.

Scripture Reference	Words and Phrases	Images
John 3:16		
1 Corinthians 13		
1 Peter 4:8		

What absolutely must be included in your video?

Who do you know or know of that you might suggest for the starring role?

Note any suggestions for colors, sounds, and setting.

Write your video notes. Feel free to use helpful sketches if you wish.

Joy

> *The world is filled with reasons to be downcast. But deeper than sorrow thrums the unbroken pulse of God's joy, a joy that will yet have its eternal day. . . . Every small experience of Jesus with us is a taste of the joy that is to come.*
>
> — ADELE ALHBERG CALHOUN

As you consider the following scriptures, note any descriptive words, phrases, and images that pop into your head.

Scripture Reference	Words and Phrases	Images
Nehemiah 8:10		
Luke 10:20		
John 15:9-11		
Acts 5:41		
Philemon 7		
1 Peter 1:8		

What absolutely must be included in your video?

Who do you know or know of that you might suggest for the starring role?

Note any suggestions for colors, sounds, and setting.

Write your video notes. Feel free to use helpful sketches if you wish.

Peace

> *First keep the peace within yourself, then you can also bring peace to others.*
>
> — THOMAS À KEMPIS

As you consider the following scriptures, note any descriptive words, phrases, and images that pop into your head.

Scripture Reference	Words and Phrases	Images
Isaiah 26:3		
John 14:27; 16:33		

Romans 8:6		
Philippians 4:7		

What absolutely must be included in your video?

Who do you know or know of that you might suggest for the starring role?

Note any suggestions for colors, sounds, and setting.

Write your video notes. Feel free to use helpful sketches if you wish.

Patience and Faithfulness

> *Faithfulness is resting in His certainty, being persuaded by His honesty, trusting in His reality, being won over by His veracity . . . being sure that He's sure and believing He's worth believing.*
>
> — BETH MOORE

As you consider the following scriptures, note any descriptive words, phrases, and images that pop into your head.

Scripture Reference	Words and Phrases	Images
1 Corinthians 13:4		
Colossians 1:10-11		
Colossians 3:13		
2 Peter 3:9		

What absolutely must be included in your video?

Who do you know or know of that you might suggest for the starring role?

Note any suggestions for colors, sounds, and setting.

Write your video notes. Feel free to use helpful sketches if you wish.

Kindness, Goodness, and Gentleness

Pour out lavishly all you have on others. You have surely far more reason for making dull sordid places bright and beautiful because of the love of your heart. No good thing will He withhold from us.

— OSWALD CHAMBERS

As you consider the following scriptures, note any descriptive words, phrases, and images that pop into your head.

Scripture Reference	Words and Phrases	Images
Ephesians 4:32		
Colossians 3:12		
Titus 3:8		
Ephesians 2:10		
Matthew 11:29		
1 Thessalonians 2:7		
1 Peter 3:4		

What absolutely must be included in your video?

Who do you know or know of that you might suggest for the starring role?

Note any suggestions for colors, sounds, and setting.

Write your video notes. Feel free to use helpful sketches if you wish.

Self-Control

Biblically, self-control is more than merely keeping in check our animal instincts and primitive urges. Its very essence is actually humility, because it has mostly to do with our minds. . . . Before it's the strength to hold yourself back, it's the ability to see, without distortion or illusion, what's really going on, and the wisdom to act in light of it.

— MARK BUCHANAN

As you consider the following scriptures, note any descriptive words, phrases, and images that pop into your head.

Scripture Reference	Words and Phrases	Images
Ephesians 4:22-24		
1 Peter 1:13-16		
1 Peter 5:6-9		

What absolutely must be included in your video?

Who do you know or know of that you might suggest for the starring role?

Note any suggestions for colors, sounds, and setting.

Write your video notes. Feel free to use helpful sketches if you wish.

Which video design is your favorite? Why?

The fruit of the Spirit, the life of God in and through us, transforms us from the inside out. It flows outward, moistening the atmosphere around us. The Spirit overflows announcing life.

What happens in you when you are bathed in Jesus' love, peace, joy, and so on? What happens to the people around you when you are bathed in Jesus' love, peace, joy, and so on?

Spend a few more minutes with Galatians 5:22-26. As you read, let the waves of abundance wash over your spirit. Then personalize the verses, forming them into a prayer.

Reflect

The Holy Spirit often uses the beauty of creation to root truth in me in such a way that it reaches deep and then bubbles up, sending out eternal ripples of life. Please consider exploring the wonder of life, growth, abundance, and overflow through one of the following exercises:

- Nurture a plant, tending it carefully and reflecting on the source of its life, on what promotes growth and health. If possible, choose a plant that produces flowers, fruit, or even herbs. Let the motion of caring for it inspire a flow of gratitude, and surrender to the Spirit's life-giving nurture of your spirit.
- Visit a greenhouse, a nursery, gardens, or an orchard regularly and use that time to reflect on the life of the Spirit within you.
- Take nature walks, noticing and reflecting on the trees along the way. Notice their root systems, sit in their shade, and see the branches reaching toward the heavens throughout each season. Let your reflection lead you to pray for healthy deep roots and a flourishing heart that overflows with life providing sustenance and shade for the weary.

Respond

You'll go out in joy,
  you'll be led into a whole and complete life.
The mountains and hills will lead the parade,
  bursting with song.
All the trees of the forest will join the procession,
  exuberant with applause.
No more thistles, but giant sequoias,
  no more thornbushes, but stately pines—

Monuments to me, to GOD,
    living and lasting evidence of GOD.
                                — ISAIAH 55:12-13, MSG

Celebrate life. Rejoice! You are not left as an orphan (see John 14:18).
The Holy Spirit has been poured out, and you will never be truly alone
again. List three ways you will go out rejoicing such as dancing in the
rain, singing, finger painting, laughing, or hugging a child.

Stand in the presence of the Spirit. Welcome and honor His presence within you and surrounding you. Step into the abundant living
waters. Feel the caress of life, get soaking wet, splash around, let the
waters cover you and quench any dryness. Become an overflowing
fountain, a living monument to God.

Please pray with me and continue to pray as you feel led:

> *Abba Father, thank You for marking me as Your child*
> *through the indwelling Holy Spirit. Thank You, Lord*
> *Jesus, for giving Your life to release living water into*
> *my life. Holy Spirit, come, flood my spirit with the*
> *abundant life of Christ. Please teach me to plunge*
> *daily into the river of life, to celebrate the wonder of*
> *belonging to an amazing God. I worship You and*
> *rejoice in Your love for me. Let me overflow with*
> *passionate love for my God that spills out wherever*
> *I go.*

Review

1. What was your initial reaction to exploring the living waters of the Spirit?
2. Which reflection exercise from weeks 1 through 3 was most meaningful for you?
3. What scripture most affected you in weeks 4 through 6?
4. What scripture was most meaningful in weeks 7 and 8?
5. What do you find most enticing about the river of life?
6. How have you experienced increased or renewed intimacy with the Spirit throughout the past eight weeks?

Notes

Week 1: Immersed in Life

1. Calvin Miller, *Celtic Devotions: A Guide to Morning and Evening Prayer* (Downers Grove, IL: InterVarsity, 2008), 27–28.

2. Dr. Bruce Demarest, *Soulguide: Following Jesus as Spiritual Director* (Colorado Springs, CO: NavPress, 2003), 62.

3. Max Lucado, *Come Thirsty: No Heart Too Dry for His Touch* (Nashville: W Publishing, 2004), 15–16.

4. Robert Jamieson, A. R. Fausset, and David Brown, *Commentary Critical and Explanatory on the Whole Bible*, www.searchgodsword .org/com/jfb/print.cgi?book=eze&chapter=047.

5. Bill T. Arnold and Bryan E. Beyer, *Encountering the Old Testament: A Christian Survey* (Grand Rapids, MI: Baker, 1999), 422.

6. C. S. Lewis, *The Silver Chair* (New York: Macmillan, 1953), 16–17.

7. Hans Kung, quoted in Rueben P. Job and Norman Shawchuck, *A Guide to Prayer for Ministers and Other Servants* (Nashville: Upper Room, 1983), 187.

8. *Secondhand Lions*, written and directed by Tim McCanlies (Burbank, CA: New Line Cinema, 2003).

9. Oswald Chambers, *My Utmost for His Highest*, ed. James Reimann (Grand Rapids, MI: Discovery House, 1992), June 13 entry.

Week 2: Running On Empty

1. *Parenthood*, directed by Ron Howard (Beverly Hills, CA: Imagine Entertainment, 1989).

2. Adele Ahlberg Calhoun, *Spiritual Disciplines Handbook: Practices That Transform Us* (Downers Grove, IL: InterVarsity, 2005), 172.

3. John Ortberg, *The Life You've Always Wanted: Spiritual Disciplines for Ordinary People* (Grand Rapids, MI: Zondervan, 2002), 189.

4. Dietrich Bonhoeffer, quoted in Jan Johnson, *Savoring God's Word: Cultivating the Soul-Transforming Practice of Scripture Meditation* (Colorado Springs, CO: NavPress, 2004), 44.

5. Mark Buchanan, *The Rest of God: Restoring Your Soul by Restoring Sabbath* (Nashville: W Publishing, 2006), 141.

6. C. S. Lewis, *The Lion, the Witch, and the Wardrobe* (New York: Collier, 1950), 160–161.

7. "Count Your Blessings," words by Johnson Oatman Jr. and music by Edwin O. Excell, 1897.

8. Jennifer Kennedy Dean, *He Restores My Soul: A Forty-Day Journey Toward Spiritual Renewal* (Nashville: Broadman, Holman, 1999), 12.

Week 3: Creating Radiance

1. David Benner, *Surrender to Love: Discovering the Heart of Christian Spirituality* (Downers Grove, IL: InterVarsity, 2003), 27.

2. Gordon MacKenzie, *Orbiting the Giant Hairball: A Corporate Fool's Guide to Surviving with Grace* (New York: Viking, 1996), 224.

3. Frances Ridley Havergal, "Take My Life and Let It Be," 1874.

Week 4: Cleansing Streams

1. David Benner, *Surrender to Love: Discovering the Heart of Christian Spirituality* (Downers Grove, IL: InterVarsity, 2003), 83.

2. Beth Moore, *Praying God's Word: Breaking Free from Spiritual Strongholds* (Nashville: Broadman, Holman, 2003), 37, 55.

3. Moore, 55.

4. Kathleen Norris, *Amazing Grace: A Vocabulary of Faith* (New York: Riverhead Books, 1998), 69–70.

5. 12Step.org: Resources and Information About the 12 Step
Program, Step 4, http://www.12step.org (accessed April 13,
2009).

6. Adele Ahlberg Calhoun, *Spiritual Disciplines Handbook: Practices
That Transform Us* (Downers Grove, IL: InterVarsity, 2005), 91.

Week 5: A Warm Bath

1. Frederick Buechner, quoted in Norman Shawchuck and Rueben
P. Job, *A Guide to Prayer for All Who Seek God* (Nashville: Upper
Room, 2003), 404.

2. Verlyn D.Verbrugge, ed., *New International Dictionary of New
Testament Theology* (Grand Rapids, MI: Zondervan, 2000), 437.

3. Verbrugge, 437.

4. John Ortberg, "Holding Out Hope," *Leadership Journal* (Fall
2008): 80.

5. Henri Nouwen, *Turn My Mourning into Dancing: Moving Through
Hard Times with Hope* (Nashville: W Publishing, 2001), 89.

Week 6: Treasures of the Deep

1. Clara H. Scott, "Open My Eyes That I May See," 1895.

2. Dallas Willard and Jan Johnson, *Renovation of the Heart in Daily
Practice: Experiments in Spiritual Transformation* (Colorado
Springs, CO: NavPress, 2006), 66.

3. Ruth Haley Barton, "Discernment: Recognizing and Responding to
the Presence of God," *Conversations* 6, no. 2 (Fall/Winter 2008): 12.

4. Elizabeth Walter, *Evidences of the Discerned Life* (Dynamics of the
Spiritual Journey, class notes, 2006).

5. Walter.

6. Jan Karon, *These High, Green Hills* (New York: Penguin Books,
1996), 88–89.

7. Richard Foster, *Celebration of Discipline: The Path to Spiritual
Growth* (New York: HarperSanFrancisco, 1998), 1.

8. Jan Johnson, *Listening to God: Using Scripture as a Path to God's*

Presence (Colorado Springs, CO: NavPress, 1998), 18.

9. Patricia Alexander and David Alexander, eds., *Eerdmans' Handbook to the Bible* (Grand Rapids, MI: Lion Publishing, 1973), 544–545.

10. Ronald A. Beers, ed., *Life Application Bible, New International Version* (Grand Rapids, MI: Zondervan and Wheaton, IL: Tyndale, 1991), 1908.

Week 7: Powerful Waters

1. Oswald Chambers, *My Utmost for His Highest* (Grand Rapids, MI: Discovery House, 1992), April 12 entry.

2. Madeleine L'Engle, *Walking on Water: Reflections on Faith and Art* (Colorado Springs, CO: Waterbrook, 2007), 82–83.

3. Charles W. Slemming, quoted in Catherine Martin, *Revive My Heart! Satisfy Your Thirst for Personal Spiritual Revival* (Colorado Springs, CO: NavPress, 2003), 28.

4. Connie Willems, "Listening Together," *Pray!* (November/December 2008): 20.

Week 8: Overflow of Life

1. Adele Ahlberg Calhoun, *Spiritual Disciplines Handbook: Practices That Transform Us* (Downers Grove, IL: InterVarsity, 2005), 26.

2. Frances Roberts, *Come Away My Beloved* (Uhrichsville, Ohio: Barbour, 2002), 50.

3. Mark Buchanan, *Hidden in Plain Sight: The Secret of More* (Nashville: Thomas Nelson, 2007), 179.

About the Author

R ita Platt is a speaker, writer, and workshop leader who focuses on delighting in and experiencing deeper relationship with God. She is passionate about knowing the Lord with her head and her heart and inspiring others to walk in intimate relationship with Him. She is currently pursuing an MA in professional counseling with an emphasis on soul care. She is a certified Prepare/Enrich premarital and marital counselor. Rita holds a BA in communication, has a certificate in women and evangelism from the Billy Graham Center, and is a trained infant-adoption liaison. She also participated in an intensive week of training at the Leighton Ford Evangelism Leadership Conference.

Rita served for years as counseling coordinator at the Colorado Springs Pregnancy Center. She wrote materials for use in training and in the counseling room, including a brochure titled *Reflections for Your Journey*, used to introduce women to the Lord. The *Reflections* brochure was translated into Russian for use in some pregnancy centers in Russia. Rita has also served in church ministry as a child and family ministry director initiating and creating new programs. She is a trained Parenting with Love and Logic facilitator and has authored articles titled "Silent Release" and "Advice for Parents of Prodigals." In addition, Rita served as worship leader for a single moms' ministry.

Rita, her husband, Thom, and Schipperke puppy, Lucy, recently relocated from Colorado Springs, Colorado, to Columbia, Maryland. Rita loves and is involved in music, performance art, and visual arts. Her hobbies include photographing waterfalls, knitting, and reading.